Trust Hacked

Trust Hacked by Nia Luckey redefines leadership for the digital age, framing trust not as a soft skill but as critical infrastructure. Drawing on her military and cybersecurity background, Nia presents the Trust Protocol, a strategic, actionable framework modeled on cybersecurity principles. The book argues that trust, like a firewall, must be systematically designed, monitored, and maintained.

Through compelling stories and practical tools, Luckey explores three core pillars: Authentication (proving credibility through consistency), Encryption (creating psychological safety), and Resilience (planning for inevitable trust breaches). She provides leaders with diagnostics, playbooks, and rituals to embed trust into daily operations, teams, and organizational culture. The final chapters address leading through AI and automation, emphasizing ethical oversight and human judgment.

Trust Hacked is a battle-tested guide for building antifragile organizations where trust is engineered to withstand pressure, recover from failure, and become a lasting competitive advantage.

Nia Luckey translates military-grade trust protocols to modern leadership. Her path was nonlinear, beginning with the exacting discipline of classical flute. That foundation in practice and precision later anchored her through very different challenges: first in the U.S. Army, where trust meant survival, and later within Fortune 500 enterprises, where its breakdown carried a different but severe cost.

Security, Audit and Leadership Series
Series Editor: Dan Swanson, Dan Swanson and Associates, Ltd.,
Winnipeg, Manitoba, Canada.

About the Book Series

The scope and mandate for cybersecurity and internal audit continues to evolve each year, as does the complexity of the business environment and speed of the changing risk landscape in which it must operate. The fundamental goal of this exciting series is to produce leading-edge books on critical subjects facing security and audit executives and practitioners. Key topics addressed include Leadership, Cybersecurity, Security Leadership, Privacy, Strategic Risk Management, Auditing IT and Technology, and Audit Management and Leadership.

Cumulative Effect: Cyber Security Guide for Directors and CEOs
By Dr Vladas Leonas

Digital Momentum: Building Real Change-Ready Enterprises
By Brice Ominski

Redefining Auditing in the Digital Era: Global Perspectives on Technology, Security, and Leadership
Edited by Abdelmounim Bouziane

Fire Brigades to Firewalls: A Public Safety Guide to Cybersecurity
By John Kuforiji

Bridging the Gap: Strengthening the Bond between Audit Committee and Internal Audit
By Denise Cicchella

CISO: Evolution of a Vocation: Confessions of a Recovering CISO
By Ron Baklarz

Dark Faces in Cyber Places: Shattering Stereotypes and Leading with Legacy in Cybersecurity
By Devon Bryan

Logic Before Language: Rethinking AI in the Age of Illusion, Bertrand Russell and the Future of Real AI
By Martin Milani

Relevant Impact: A Field Guide to Integrated Assurance
By Patrick M. Hayes

Cybersecurity and the Art of Cyberwar
By Dan Shoemaker, Tamara Shoemaker, and Amir Jabri

Trust Hacked: What Firewalls, Failures, and the Frontlines Taught Me About Trust
By Nia Luckey

Trust Hacked

What Firewalls, Failures, and the Frontlines Taught Me About Trust

Nia Luckey

CRC Press
Taylor & Francis Group
Boca Raton London New York

CRC Press is an imprint of the
Taylor & Francis Group, an **informa** business

Designed cover image: Shutterstock ID: 2292609361

First edition published 2027
by CRC Press
2385 NW Executive Center Drive, Suite 320, Boca Raton FL 33431

and by CRC Press
4 Park Square, Milton Park, Abingdon, Oxon, OX14 4RN

CRC Press is an imprint of Taylor & Francis Group, LLC

ISBN: 978-1-041-17266-6 (hbk)
ISBN: 978-1-041-17267-3 (pbk)
ISBN: 978-1-003-68881-5 (ebk)

DOI: 10.1201/9781003688815

Typeset in Caslon
by KnowledgeWorks Global Ltd.

Contents

About the Author

Nia Luckey translates military-grade trust protocols to modern leadership. Her path was nonlinear, beginning with the exacting discipline of classical flute. That foundation in practice and precision later anchored her through very different challenges: first in the U.S. Army, where trust meant survival, and later within Fortune 500 enterprises, where its breakdown carried a different but severe cost.

Across these worlds, she observed a common vulnerability. Organizations often treat trust as a cultural bonus or a personal trait. Nia recognized it as operational infrastructure, as critical and as designable as any technical system. This insight became the Trust Protocol, a field-tested framework that helps leaders engineer resilience, safety, and credibility into their teams and processes.

Her work is driven by a simple conviction forged through experience: the systems we build are only as strong as the human trust that powers them. *Trust Hacked* provides the blueprint.

Nia advises leaders, speaks on building antifragile organizations, and is a committed advocate for veterans and women in leadership.

Preface

There is no straight line to purpose. Only the courage to keep walking when the path bends and the light fades. My journey has never been the traditional one. It was uneven, unpredictable, and at times, unfinished. I did not begin in boardrooms or technology labs. I began my service in the U.S. Army, learning to lead with conviction, adapt with urgency, and listen with intent. Those lessons became my foundation long before I ever stepped into cybersecurity.

Every experience, whether military, corporate, academic, or personal, has shaped the person I am today. I often reminded myself during the hardest moments:

> "The moments that break you are often the ones building you for what comes next."

It is a truth I have lived, not just believed.

Cybersecurity, for me, has always been more than a profession. It reflects how I see the world, a constant pursuit of trust, accountability, and protection. Systems, like people, need both structure and compassion. And when trust is fractured, the goal is not to rebuild barriers. It is to rebuild belief.

> "Technology will evolve, threats will adapt, but integrity, empathy, and connection will always be our strongest defense."

That same belief has guided me far beyond my professional world. Through nonprofit work, mentoring, and community outreach, I have learned that giving back is not what you do once you have achieved success. It is how you define it. Every veteran I have met, every woman I have mentored, every student I have encouraged has reaffirmed a truth I hold close.

> "Leadership is not about being seen. It is about seeing others clearly enough to lift them higher."

Still, my journey is far from perfect. I am not perfect. I do not know everything, nor do I strive to be the smartest person in the room. I am humbled and honored to be in rooms full of brilliant minds, to learn, to listen, and to grow among them. Every chapter of my life has been written by collaboration, by curiosity, and by the courage to admit that growth is never done.

This book is written in reverence of those whose presence built my strength and whose absence deepened my resolve. To my beloved mother, Stella Sigal, whose grace and endurance continue to guide my spirit. To my brother, Anthony Chiaraluce, whose unwavering belief in me remains a light in dark places. To my uncle, Steven DiMare, whose quiet wisdom taught me that authentic leadership begins with humility. To my grandparents, who laid the foundation of my resilience and faith. To Ruben Rios, a Marine and kindred spirit in service, your honor, discipline, and sacrifice remind me that courage endures beyond time.

And to Sophie Elden, my grandmother and heart. Your life was a painful reflection of what the world does to those it does not understand. Yet your strength, even in silence, became my own. I carry you with me in every space where compassion and courage are required.

This book is also a living tribute to my family, my husband, Jesse Luckey, and our children, Aden Coombs, Laehla Luckey, and Adalina Luckey. You are the reason behind every late night, every leap of faith, and every step forward.

> "When your purpose feels unclear, look at the faces that ground you. There you will find your why."

If there is one truth that has carried me through, it is this. Resilience is not about never falling. It is about learning how to rise with grace, intention, and gratitude. Every chapter that follows was written from that place.

As you read these pages, I hope you do not just find lessons about cybersecurity or leadership. I hope you find yourself reflected here, too. Because your story, however imperfect or unconventional, has value. Your path matters. And the moments you think are detours might be destiny in disguise. The following is a story of stories; all characters and scenarios are fictitious. Any resemblance to real persons, living or dead, is purely coincidental.

~Nia Luckey

AI Statement

This manuscript used automated tools to support accessibility, visual development, and editorial refinement. OpenAI's ChatGPT (GPT-5.2) was used to draft and refine image accessibility descriptions (alt text).

Grammarly (version 14.x, current at time of use) was used throughout the manuscript for grammar, style, and readability suggestions.

OpenAI's Sora 2 (latest publicly released video generation model as of September 2025) and associated Sora generation tools were used to create three conceptual figures—The Trust Protocol (Figure I.1), The TIRS Response Cycle (Figure 3.1), and The Vulnerability Map (Trust Protocol Diagnostic Tool (Figure 4.1)). The images are explicitly based on author-provided descriptions and iterative refinement. All outputs were reviewed, edited, and approved by the author, who retains full responsibility for the final content, visuals, accuracy, and interpretations presented.

INTRODUCTION

Trust Is the Hidden Vulnerability

It was well past midnight when the glow of my GPS screen became my lifeline. I had been on the road for nearly twelve hours, driving from North Carolina to Connecticut. Fatigue pressed against me like a weight, and the only thing pulling me forward was the thought of finally making it home. The interstate had been my companion for most of the trip, predictable, steady, and well-lit. As I entered New York City, the rhythm changed.

"Exit right," the voice instructed.

I listened and acted without hesitation. After so many hours, the commands had become instinctive, almost automatic. But the moment I left the safety of the highway, the landscape around me shifted. The streets narrowed, the light thinned, and by the time I reached the first stoplight, the GPS gave its following command.

"Turn left."

I looked to my left and froze. It was not a road that inspired confidence. It was a dark alleyway, barely illuminated by a single flickering streetlamp. The streets were barren, tranquil for a city that never sleeps. The shadows stretched long, and the silence was heavier than the darkness itself.

For a split second, exhaustion tempted me to comply. I was too tired to think critically, too worn down from the twelve-hour journey to question a system that had guided me across multiple states without fail. My hands twitched on the steering wheel as if ready to turn, as tears began to fall from my eyes.

But then another thought cut through the fog: What if I was wrong to trust this?

I pulled over, heart pounding, and called my uncle. My voice carried a mix of embarrassment and unease as I explained what the GPS had told me to do. He did not hesitate. "You're okay," he said calmly,

DOI: 10.1201/9781003688815-1

"we just need to get you back on the highway." His words steadied me as he gave directions that pulled me out of that dark, unfamiliar maze and back onto the route I needed.

That night has never left me, not because of where I was, but because of what it revealed. Until that moment, I had not realized how much trust I had placed in a system I did not understand. Satellites, algorithms, and updates were invisible to me, yet I had surrendered my judgment to them without question. If the GPS said, "turn left," I was conditioned to believe it knew better than I did, even when common sense suggested otherwise, an unsettling realization.

Trust rarely breaks in dramatic, headline-making failures. More often, it falters in small, ordinary decisions: whether to follow a glowing arrow on a screen, whether to believe a system's output, whether to obey without pausing to think. That dark alleyway was more than a wrong turn. It was a glimpse into the fragility of trust.

What haunted me was not the possibility of making a wrong turn in New York City. It was how quickly I had been willing to follow, even when my instincts told me otherwise. It showed me how invisible the contracts we make with our technology can be. You guide me, and I will follow. I will not question how you know or why you are certain. I will believe.

That was the night I began to understand that the most fragile infrastructure we have is not our roads, our wires, or even our data. It is trust.

Why "Turn Left" Is a Metaphor for Leadership Decisions

That night in New York, staring down a dark alley, I realized how quickly trust could override instinct. The words "turn left" had carried so much authority that I nearly surrendered my judgment without question. The more I thought about it later, the more I realized how often leaders face similar moments.

In the military, we were trained to trust systems, procedures, and, most importantly, each other. Orders mattered because lives depended on them. Yet even in that environment, we were taught that blind trust could be dangerous. Following an instruction without assessing context could lead to unnecessary risk or failure. The best leaders were those who could pause in that critical second, weigh the data against their instincts, and decide whether to follow the command or adjust their course.

"Turn left" became a metaphor for leadership decisions. Leaders are often asked to make decisive moves in complex environments. They receive directives from systems, advisors, and processes that claim authority. In many cases, those directives are right. But in moments of ambiguity, when the road ahead looks nothing like what is described, the easy choice is to obey without question. The harder option is to pause, test, and consider whether the decision aligns with reality.

During deployments, I saw firsthand how trust operated as both an asset and a liability. A unit functions effectively only when trust is strong; yet misplaced trust can endanger the mission. If intelligence reported that a route was clear, we wanted to believe it. But good leaders are verified. They asked questions, scanned the horizon, and prepared contingencies. They understood that trust must be earned and maintained, not assumed.

The civilian world is not so different. A team member may trust a leader's decision to pivot strategy or to implement a new system. An organization may trust its data models to predict future performance. A society may trust its institutions to safeguard rights and resources. In each case, there is a "turn left" moment: the instant where trust is tested against judgment.

The problem is that many of us, whether in boardrooms, operations centers, or cultural initiatives, have been conditioned to follow authority unquestioningly. We equate confidence with correctness. We equate process with truth. And so, like me that night, we find ourselves at a stoplight staring at a dark alley, rationalizing why it might still be safe to turn.

Authentic leadership demands something different. It requires the courage to pause, to resist the automatic response, and to acknowledge that trust without verification is a form of vulnerability. Leaders who understand this do not diminish trust; they strengthen it. They create cultures where questioning is not seen as disobedience, but as a sign of diligence. They model decision-making that combines trust in systems with awareness of their limits.

That is why "turn left" has stayed with me. It is not just a reminder of a late-night drive gone wrong. It is a symbol of the leadership challenge we all face: the tension between speed and reflection, between reliance and responsibility, between trusting the system and trusting ourselves.

The Trust Breakdown in Tech, Teams, and Institutions

In the military, trust is not a philosophical ideal. It is a matter of survival. You trust the soldier to your left and right, the system guiding your mission, and the chain of command that directs it. If any of those layers fail, consequences are immediate and irreversible. That experience shaped my understanding of trust as both a personal responsibility and a structural necessity. It isn't optional. It is the hidden infrastructure on which everything else depends.

Yet in the civilian and corporate world, I quickly noticed how differently trust was treated. It was often spoken of as a "soft skill," something to aspire to rather than a baseline requirement. When an organization lacks trust, whether in its systems or in its leadership, it begins to fracture in subtle yet dangerous ways. Employees disengage. Customers doubt. Partners hesitate.

We are living in a moment where trust in technology, institutions, and leadership is under unprecedented strain. Consider the events of early 2024, when a central AI platform suffered a systemic failure that disrupted financial transactions across multiple countries for nearly 48 hours. Billions of dollars in payments were delayed, payroll systems halted, and global trade routes stalled. The technical error was complex but solvable. The real crisis came from the collapse of confidence. Companies questioned whether they could rely on AI-driven infrastructure. Consumers flooded social media with panic, unsure if their savings or transactions would ever recover. Regulators demanded immediate answers, but were met with silence.

What unfolded was not just a technical outage. It was a trust outage. The technology eventually came back online, but the faith in its reliability did not return as easily. Investors pulled out of key markets. Governments fast-tracked oversight. Startups dependent on the failed platform were forced to close. What crumbled that week was not just code, it was confidence.

This is the same pattern I recognized that night in New York when my GPS let me down, only on a global scale. A system we trusted implicitly failed without warning, and because we had no tools to question or verify its guidance, chaos followed. Whether on the road, on the battlefield, or in the boardroom, when trust breaks down, the damage spreads faster than the technical issue itself.

The breakdown extends beyond technology. In organizations across various industries, leaders are grappling with trust deficits that manifest in measurable ways, including decreased productivity, increased turnover, failed initiatives, and compromised innovation. Teams that once collaborated seamlessly now second-guess decisions. Employees who once embraced change now resist it. Customers who once advocated for brands now question their motives.

The pattern is consistent: when trust erodes, everything else becomes exponentially more difficult. Communication requires more effort. Decisions take longer. Recovery from setbacks becomes nearly impossible. What should be routine operations become complex negotiations. What should be strategic advantages become operational liabilities.

This is not a crisis of technology or leadership alone. It is an infrastructure crisis; the invisible foundation that enables everything else to function. When trust fails, it reveals how dependent we have become on systems, processes, and relationships that we never fully understood or verified. We built our operations on assumptions of reliability that were never tested until they broke.

That is why reframing trust as infrastructure is so urgent. In the digital age, trust extends beyond human relationships. It resides in algorithms, contracts, leadership decisions, and the invisible systems we use to navigate our lives. When those systems are opaque, unaccountable, or brittle, trust becomes the hidden vulnerability that no firewall can defend against.

Why Trust Isn't a Soft Skill (and Never Was)

Trust is often described as a soft skill, something intangible or optional. Experience shows this is a dangerous misconception. The GPS failure in New York, my military deployments, and the 2024 AI outage all demonstrate that trust functions as infrastructure. It carries critical weight. It enables decisions, governs reliance on systems, and sustains operations. When trust fails, the consequences are immediate and measurable.

In the military, trust is operational. Soldiers depend on each other, on communication systems, and on procedures to achieve objectives. A breakdown in trust does not simply affect morale. It can compromise an entire mission. Trust is reinforced through accountability, shared standards, and repeated verification. These are not optional; they are essential for functioning teams.

The immediate problem is technical, and the broader impact is a potential collapse of confidence. The 2024 AI platform failure disrupted global financial transactions for nearly 48 hours. The immediate problem was technical, but the broader impact was a collapse of confidence. Investors, regulators, and customers questioned whether systems could be relied upon. Trust here was quantifiable. It affected revenue, operational continuity, and reputational risk. The lesson is clear: trust is measurable, actionable, and directly linked to performance outcomes.

Organizations often treat trust as a cultural nicety rather than an operational imperative. Teams are rewarded for output, leaders are evaluated on efficiency, and technology is judged on functionality. Yet all of these systems rely on trust to operate effectively. Trust ensures that people follow guidance correctly, that systems are used reliably, and that decisions are executed as intended. Without it, even the most sophisticated operations fail.

Consider the metrics that matter in any organization: employee retention, customer satisfaction, operational efficiency, innovation velocity, and crisis recovery time. Trust levels directly influence each of these. High-trust organizations consistently outperform their peers across these measures. Low-trust organizations struggle with basic functions, regardless of their technical capabilities or strategic advantages.

Trust affects decision speed. In high-trust environments, decisions can be made quickly because verification processes are streamlined and confidence in execution is high. In low-trust environments, every decision requires extensive validation, multiple approvals, and contingency planning. The operational cost is significant and measurable.

Trust affects resource allocation. High-trust teams can operate with leaner oversight, fewer redundant systems, and more efficient communication channels. Low-trust teams require additional management layers, more frequent check-ins, and backup systems. The resource drain is quantifiable and ongoing.

Trust affects innovation capacity. High-trust cultures encourage experimentation, rapid iteration, and intelligent risk-taking. Low-trust cultures default to conservative approaches, extensive documentation, and risk avoidance. The competitive impact is explicit and cumulative.

Trust is not a soft skill. It is a capability that must be designed, maintained, and measured. It is a discipline that blends human judgment, technological reliability, and organizational accountability. Like any other infrastructure, it can be strengthened, tested, and repaired. Leaders who treat trust as optional are exposed to hidden vulnerabilities. Those who treat it as essential create resilience, confidence, and lasting performance.

The experiences on the highway, in the field, and across global technology failures all converge on this point. Trust must be treated with the same rigor as strategy, technology, and leadership in military, corporate, or societal environments. It is foundational, tangible, and operational. To succeed in any setting, trust must be deliberately built, maintained, and safeguarded.

Overview of the Trust Protocol

The realization that trust functions as infrastructure led me to a critical question: If trust is this essential, why don't we have systematic approaches to building, maintaining, and protecting it? We have cybersecurity protocols, project management frameworks, and quality assurance methodologies. Yet when it comes to trust, the foundation that enables all other systems to function, most organizations rely on intuition, good intentions, and hope.

This gap became the catalyst for developing the Trust Protocol™, a strategic framework that applies the same rigor to trust that we use to enterprise cybersecurity. The parallel is not accidental. Both trust and cybersecurity are invisible until they fail. Both require proactive design rather than reactive response. Both demand continuous monitoring, regular updates, and systematic maintenance. And both, when compromised, can bring down entire operations regardless of other strengths.

The Trust Protocol™ is built on three foundational principles that mirror the core elements of cybersecurity architecture:

Authentication addresses the question of identity and credibility. In cybersecurity, authentication verifies that users are who they claim to be before granting access to systems. In trust, authentication establishes leadership presence, consistency, and reliability. It ensures that leaders can be counted on to act in alignment with their stated values and commitments. Authentication in trust means that your identity as a leader is verified through consistent actions, transparent communication, and reliable follow-through. It is the foundation that allows others to engage with your leadership confidently.

Encryption protects sensitive information during transmission and storage. In trust, encryption creates psychological safety, maintains confidentiality, and establishes clear cultural boundaries. It ensures that sensitive conversations, vulnerable admissions, and strategic discussions can happen without fear of misuse or exposure. Encryption in trust means creating environments where people can communicate openly, share concerns honestly, and collaborate without fear that their contributions will be weaponized against them.

Resilience prepares systems to withstand attacks, recover from breaches, and maintain operations during disruptions. In trust, resilience involves being prepared for trust failures, responding systematically to breaches, and planning structured recovery. It acknowledges that trust will be tested, damaged, and sometimes broken, and it provides frameworks for restoration and strengthening. Resilience in trust means having protocols for addressing mistakes, repairing relationships, and emerging stronger from conflicts or failures.

The Trust Protocol™ is not a metaphor; it is a strategic infrastructure model designed for leaders who operate at the intersection of human dynamics and systems thinking. It recognizes that modern leadership requires the same systematic approach to trust that we apply to technology, security, and operations. It provides decision-ready tools, measurable outcomes, and scalable processes.

Throughout this book, the Trust Protocol™ framework is reinforced with real-world scenarios, practical use cases, and actionable strategies. Each principle is explored in depth, including specific implementation techniques, measurement metrics, and methods for continuous improvement. The goal is not just to understand trust as infrastructure, but to build, maintain, and protect it with the same discipline we apply to any other critical system.

The Trust Protocol™ emerges from the recognition that trust is too important to be left to chance. In an era where technology failures can cascade globally within hours, organizational changes occur at unprecedented speed, and leadership decisions have immediate and far-reaching consequences, trust cannot be treated as a soft skill or a mere cultural aspiration. It must be engineered, monitored, and maintained as the critical infrastructure it has always been.

This is not about making trust more technical or less human. It is about making trust more reliable, more resilient, and better able to support the complex demands of modern leadership. The Trust Protocol™ provides the framework for leaders who understand that trust is not just nice to have; it is the hidden infrastructure that determines whether everything else succeeds or fails.

The journey from that dark alley in New York to the development of the Trust Protocol™ has been one of recognizing that our most critical vulnerabilities are often the ones we cannot see. Trust is invisible until it breaks. But with the proper framework, it can be built to last, designed to scale, and maintained to perform when it matters most.

Throughout this book, we explore how to implement the Trust Protocol across contexts, from individual leadership development to organizational transformation and societal resilience. The framework is adaptable, measurable, and practical. Most importantly, it is necessary. Because in a world where everything is connected, trust is not just the foundation; it is the entire structure that holds everything else together (Figure I.1).

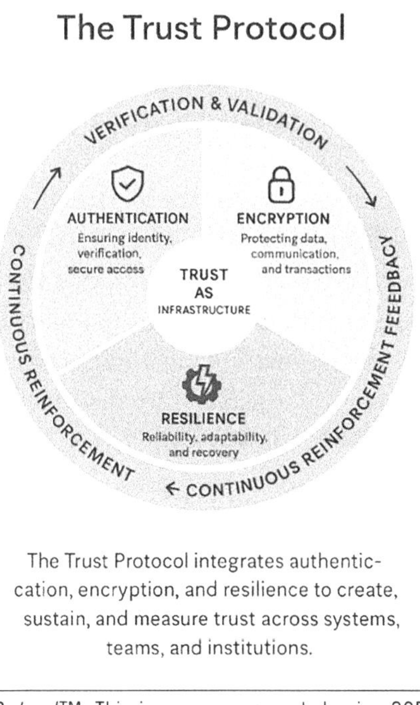

Figure I.1 *The Trust Protocol*™. This image was generated using SORA (AI image-generation tool) in Q4 2025 and selected by the author for conceptual accuracy and analytical clarity).

1

Why Everything Breaks Without Trust

In the early hours of March 15, 2019, a junior cybersecurity analyst at a Fortune 500 financial services company noticed something unusual. The network monitoring dashboard showed an anomalous pattern of data transfers occurring during off-peak hours. The signature appeared suspicious. Small, consistent packets were directed to an external IP address not on any approved vendor list. The protocol dictated that she should immediately escalate this to her supervisor.

She hesitated.

Three weeks earlier, she had flagged what she thought was a similar anomaly, only to discover it was a legitimate backup process that IT had failed to document appropriately. Her supervisor had publicly questioned her judgment in the next team meeting, suggesting she needed to "think before crying wolf." The embarrassment still stung. Instead of immediately escalating, she spent 2 hours verifying the traffic herself by cross-referencing logs and running additional scans.

By the time she finally escalated the alert, the attackers had already exfiltrated 2.3 million customer records.

The post-incident analysis later revealed that the breach could have been contained within minutes if the initial alert had been acted on immediately. The technical systems worked perfectly, the monitoring tools detected the intrusion, the alerts fired correctly, and the response protocols were sound. What failed was trust. A junior employee's trust in her leadership, her confidence in speaking up, and the team's collective trust in each other's judgment.

This is the hidden vulnerability in every organization: the human trust layer that sits beneath all our technical defenses. While we spend billions on firewalls, encryption, and monitoring systems, we often ignore the most critical component of our security infrastructure.

DOI: 10.1201/9781003688815-2

These trust relationships determine whether those systems actually work when it matters most.

The Anatomy of a Breach: What Mistrust Looks Like

When cybersecurity professionals conduct post-incident analyses, they typically focus on technical failures, such as unpatched systems, misconfigured firewalls, or sophisticated attack vectors. But dig deeper into the timeline of any significant breach, and you'll find a pattern of human hesitation, communication breakdowns, and trust failures that created the conditions for technical systems to fail.

Consider the 2017 Equifax breach, one of the most devastating data breaches in history. While the technical cause was a known Apache Struts vulnerability that went unpatched, the human factors tell a more complex story. The vulnerability had been identified, and a patch was available; however, the information didn't flow effectively throughout the organization. Teams were working in silos, communication protocols were unclear, and there was insufficient trust in the urgency of security updates versus business continuity concerns.

The breach wasn't just a technical failure; it was a failure of the trust system. Multiple people had the necessary information to prevent the breach. Still, the organizational trust infrastructure wasn't robust enough to ensure that critical information flowed to the right people at the right time with the appropriate level of urgency.

This pattern repeats across industries and breach types. In healthcare, we see medical errors that occur not because of a lack of knowledge, but because junior staff don't feel safe challenging senior physicians. In aviation, accidents happen when co-pilots don't feel empowered to question captains. In the financial services industry, fraud often goes undetected because employees fear retaliation for raising concerns about powerful clients or colleagues.

The anatomy of organizational failure almost always includes a trust pathology: someone knew something was wrong, but the trust infrastructure wasn't strong enough to ensure that knowledge translated into action.

Fear, Silence, and Ignored Alerts

In cybersecurity, we have a concept called "alert fatigue," in which security teams become overwhelmed by the volume of alerts and begin to ignore or deprioritize them. But there's another type of alert fatigue that's far more dangerous: human alert fatigue, where people stop raising concerns because they've learned that speaking up is costly, ineffective, or hazardous to their careers.

This human alert fatigue manifests in several ways:

The Cassandra Complex: Named after the Greek mythological figure who was cursed to prophesy the truth but never be believed, this occurs when employees repeatedly raise legitimate concerns that are dismissed or ignored. Over time, these employees either stop raising concerns altogether or leave the organization, taking their institutional knowledge and risk awareness with them.

Hierarchical Silence: In organizations with steep power gradients, information flows upward poorly. Junior employees often identify problems that senior leaders overlook, but the cultural and structural barriers to upward communication prevent critical intelligence from reaching decision-makers. This is particularly dangerous in rapidly changing environments, where ground-level employees often have the most up-to-date information on emerging risks.

Silo Blindness: When teams operate in isolation, each group may have pieces of a larger puzzle, but no one has the trust relationships necessary to share information across boundaries. Marketing may be aware of customer complaints that indicate a security issue, but they don't trust or communicate with IT. Operations might notice unusual patterns that could indicate fraud, but they don't have relationships with the compliance team.

Retaliation Fear: Perhaps the most toxic form of trust breakdown, this occurs when employees have learned through experience or observation that raising concerns leads to negative consequences. They may be labeled as "not team players," passed over for promotions, or even terminated. Once this pattern is established, it creates a culture of willful blindness in which everyone knows problems exist, but no one is willing to name them.

The cybersecurity parallel is instructive here. In well-designed security systems, we assume that individual components will fail, so we build in redundancy, monitoring, and fail-safes. We don't rely on a single firewall or detection system; we build layered defenses with multiple points of detection and response.

But in human systems, we often rely on single points of failure. We assume that the right person will speak up, that information will flow naturally, and that people will overcome social and political barriers to do the right thing. We don't build redundancy into our trust systems, nor do we create fail-safes for when trust breaks down.

The Cost of Team Hesitation

The financial cost of trust breakdowns is staggering, but it's often hidden in metrics we don't typically associate with trust. Consider these scenarios:

Decision Latency: When teams don't trust each other's judgment or expertise, decision-making slows dramatically. Every choice requires additional validation, more meetings, and higher-level approval. In fast-moving markets or a crisis, this latency can be fatal. A cybersecurity team that doesn't trust its threat intelligence might spend days validating an alert that requires immediate action. A product team that doesn't trust its user research might delay a critical feature release while conducting additional studies.

Redundant Verification: In low-trust environments, work gets done multiple times. Teams independently verify information they don't trust from other teams, consultants are hired to validate internal recommendations, and parallel processes emerge because groups don't trust each other's work. This isn't just inefficient; it's a high hidden cost to organizational productivity.

Innovation Paralysis: Trust is the foundation of intelligent risk-taking. When teams don't trust that failures will be treated as learning opportunities, they become risk-averse to the point of paralysis. They choose safe, incremental improvements over breakthrough innovations. They wait for perfect information instead of making intelligent bets. They optimize for not being wrong rather than for being right.

Talent Hemorrhaging: High-performing employees are often the first to recognize trust breakdowns and the most likely to have options elsewhere. When trust erodes, organizations not only lose productivity but also their best people, along with their institutional knowledge, relationships, and capabilities.

The cybersecurity analogy here is "defense in depth": the idea that security should be layered, with multiple independent systems providing protection. When one layer fails, others should still offer protection. But in human systems, trust failures often cascade. When people lose trust in leadership, they also lose trust in the organization's mission, their colleagues' competence, and their own ability to make a difference.

Lessons from Cyber Incidents

The cybersecurity field has developed sophisticated frameworks for understanding and responding to incidents. The NIST Cybersecurity Framework, for example, provides a structured approach to Identify, Protect, Detect, Respond, and Recover from cyber threats. These frameworks are effective because they assume incidents will occur and focus on developing systems to prevent, detect, and recover from failures.

We can apply these same principles to trust systems:

Identify: Just as cybersecurity teams maintain asset inventories and risk assessments, leaders need to identify their trusted assets and vulnerabilities. Who are the key trust nodes in your organization? What are the critical trust relationships that, if broken, would cause systemic failure? Where are your trust single points of failure?

Protect: Cybersecurity teams implement controls to prevent incidents. Similarly, leaders need to implement trust-control systems, processes, and cultural practices to protect against trust erosion. This might include regular feedback mechanisms, transparent decision-making processes, and clear escalation paths for concerns.

Detect: Security systems include monitoring and alerting to detect incidents in real time. Trust systems need similar tracking. What are the early warning signs of trust breakdown? How do you detect when communication is breaking down, when people are hesitating to speak up, or when silos are forming?

Respond: When security incidents occur, teams follow established response procedures. Trust incidents need similar response protocols. How do you respond when trust is broken? What are the steps for investigating trust failures, communicating about them, and beginning recovery?

Recover: Security teams focus on restoring systems and improving defenses after incidents. Trust recovery requires a similar systematic approach. It's not just about apologizing or moving on, but about rebuilding the systems and relationships that have failed.

The most sophisticated cybersecurity programs also include "red team" exercises. Allowing teams to run simulated attacks is designed to test defenses and identify weaknesses before real attackers do. Organizations need similar "trust red team" exercises. These exercises would bridge the gaps between human resources (HR) and Insider Threat programs, providing structured ways to test their trust systems under stress and identify vulnerabilities before they lead to real failures.

Defining the Tool: Beyond Traditional Approaches

Before we dive deeper into specific trust vulnerabilities and defenses, it's essential to understand how this approach differs from traditional leadership and organizational development tools. Most leadership frameworks focus either on individual traits (emotional intelligence, communication skills, decision-making) or on macro-organizational factors (culture, strategy, structure). This book takes a different approach, treating trust as a technical system that can be designed, implemented, monitored, and maintained.

Think of it this way: traditional leadership development is like teaching someone to drive well, focusing on skills, judgment, and behavior. This approach is akin to teaching someone to design and maintain the entire transportation infrastructure; the roads, traffic signals, safety systems, and protocols that enable safe driving at scale.

This isn't to diminish the importance of individual leadership skills, but rather to recognize that in complex organizations, personal excellence isn't sufficient. You need systems that work even when individuals make mistakes, have bad days, or leave the organization. You need infrastructure that supports informed decision-making and identifies problems before they escalate into crises.

The cybersecurity analogy is particularly apt because cybersecurity professionals have learned to think systematically about human factors. They don't just focus on technical controls; they design systems that consider human psychology, social dynamics, and organizational pressures. They assume that people will make mistakes, that attackers will exploit human vulnerabilities, and that technical systems must be designed to work within human limitations.

These same systems of thinking can be applied to trust. Instead of relying on leaders to be trustworthy and expecting employees to trust them, we can design organizational systems that increase the likelihood of trust, detect trust issues early, and recover quickly when trust is compromised.

Fear, Silence, and Ignored Alerts: The Human Vulnerability Layer

In cybersecurity, we often refer to the "human layer" as the weakest link in security systems. Phishing attacks succeed not because of technical vulnerabilities, but because they exploit human psychology. Social engineering is practical because attackers exploit trust, authority, and social dynamics to gain access to sensitive information.

But humans aren't just a vulnerability; they're also the most sophisticated detection-and-response system we have. Humans can recognize patterns that automated systems often miss, adapt to novel situations, and make complex judgments that require a deep understanding of context. The goal isn't to eliminate human judgment from security systems, but to create systems that amplify human strengths while compensating for human weaknesses.

The same principle applies to organizational trust systems. People are both the most significant vulnerability and the greatest asset in trust systems. They can detect subtle changes in organizational dynamics, recognize emerging problems, and adapt to new situations. But they're also subject to cognitive biases, social pressures, and emotional reactions that can compromise their judgment.

Consider the phenomenon of "normalization of deviance," a concept developed by sociologist Diane Vaughan to explain how organizations gradually accept lower standards of performance until failure becomes inevitable. This happened at NASA before the Challenger disaster, when engineers gradually came to accept higher levels of risk as usual. It happens in financial institutions before fraud scandals, where questionable practices become routine. It often occurs in healthcare systems before patient safety crises, where workarounds and shortcuts become standard practices.

Normalization of deviance is fundamentally a failure of the trust system. It occurs when the feedback loops that should detect and correct problems break down. People stop raising concerns because they've learned that concerns aren't welcomed or acted upon. Leaders stop hearing about problems because their teams have learned not to bring them bad news. The organization's immune system, its ability to detect and respond to threats, becomes compromised.

The Cost of Team Hesitation: Quantifying Trust Failures

While trust breakdowns are often discussed in abstract terms, their costs are measurable and substantial. Research by the Harvard Business School found that employees in high-trust organizations are 76% more engaged, 50% more productive, and 40% less likely to experience burnout. They also take 13% fewer sick days and are 76% more likely to recommend their company to others.

But these aggregate statistics don't capture the acute costs of trust failures in critical moments. Consider these scenarios:

The Hesitation Tax: In a software development team, a junior developer notices what appears to be a security vulnerability in code written by a senior team member. However, the senior developer has a reputation for being defensive about feedback, and the junior developer isn't entirely sure about the issue. They spend two days researching and testing before raising the concern, during which time the vulnerable code is deployed to production. The two-day delay turns a simple fix into a complex rollback-and-patch process, incurring $50,000 in downtime and emergency response costs for the company.

The Silence Penalty: In a manufacturing facility, a line worker notices that a safety protocol isn't consistently followed, but previous attempts to raise safety concerns have been met with dismissal or blame. The worker stays silent, and three weeks later, an accident occurs that could have been prevented. The resulting injury, investigation, and regulatory response cost the company $2 million and damaged its reputation with both customers and employees.

The Verification Overhead: In a consulting firm, teams often duplicate each other's work because they lack confidence in the quality or completeness of work across teams. Multiple groups independently verify client deliverables, research is repeated, and recommendations are second-guessed. This hidden redundancy adds 30% to project costs and delays delivery timelines, making the firm less competitive and less profitable.

These aren't hypothetical scenarios; they're patterns that play out daily in organizations around the world. The cybersecurity field has developed sophisticated methods for calculating the cost of security incidents, including direct expenses (such as response, recovery, and fines) and indirect costs (such as reputation damage, customer churn, and regulatory scrutiny). We need similar frameworks for calculating the cost of trust incidents.

Lessons from Cyber Incidents: Building Antifragile Trust Systems

The cybersecurity field has evolved from a reactive, incident-response model to a proactive, resilience-focused approach. Modern cybersecurity isn't just about preventing attacks, but also about building systems that can detect, contain, and recover from attacks quickly and effectively. The assumption is that attacks will succeed, so the focus is on minimizing damage and learning from each incident to strengthen defenses.

This evolution offers essential lessons for trust systems. Instead of trying to prevent all trust breakdowns, we should focus on building systems that can detect trust problems early, contain their damage, and recover quickly while learning from each incident.

Assume Breach: In cybersecurity, the "assume breach" principle is fundamental: design systems assuming attackers will eventually gain access. For trust systems, this means trust will occasionally break down, and that designing systems that can function even when trust is imperfect is essential. This might include decision-making processes that don't rely on perfect information sharing, escalation procedures that work even when normal communication channels fail, and recovery protocols that can rebuild trust after it's been damaged.

Defense in Depth: Cybersecurity systems employ multiple layers of protection, ensuring that if one layer fails, others remain intact. Trust systems need similar layering. Don't rely solely on individual relationships. Build institutional trust through transparent processes, clear policies, and consistent enforcement. Don't rely exclusively on formal communication channels; create informal networks and alternative pathways for information to flow.

Continuous Monitoring: Modern cybersecurity includes constant monitoring and real-time threat detection. Trust systems need similar monitoring capabilities. What are the leading indicators of trust breakdown? How do you detect when communication is becoming less effective, when people are becoming more hesitant to speak up, or when silos are forming? Regular pulse surveys, exit interviews, and 360-degree feedback can provide some monitoring, but organizations need more sophisticated, real-time approaches.

Incident Response: When cybersecurity incidents occur, teams follow established playbooks that define roles, responsibilities, and procedures. Trust incidents need similar response protocols when trust breaks down. Whether due to a leadership failure, a communication breakdown, or a policy violation, there should be clear procedures in place for investigating the incident, communicating about it, and initiating the recovery process.

Threat Intelligence: Cybersecurity teams share threat and vulnerability information across organizations and industries. Trust systems could benefit from similar intelligence sharing. What are the typical patterns of trust breakdown? What early warning signs should leaders watch for? How can organizations learn from each other's trust failures and successes?

Tool: Trust Breakdown Checklist

Drawing from cybersecurity incident response frameworks, here's a diagnostic tool for identifying and assessing trust breakdowns in your organization:

Detection Indicators:

- Increased decision latency (decisions taking longer than usual)
- Decreased voluntary information sharing across teams
- Increased formal escalations and decreased informal problem-solving
- Higher turnover among high-performing employees
- Decreased participation in meetings and collaborative activities
- Increased use of email/documentation for communications that were previously handled verbally
- More frequent requests for "confirmation in writing."
- Decreased innovation and increased risk aversion
- Increased complaints to HR or external parties
- Decreased customer satisfaction scores related to service coordination

Assessment Questions:

1. **Information Flow** Are people receiving the necessary information to perform their jobs effectively? Are there any delays or gaps in the sharing of critical information?
2. **Escalation Patterns:** Are problems being escalated appropriately, or are people either over-escalating (due to lack of confidence) or under-escalating (due to fear of consequences)?
3. **Decision Quality:** Are decisions being made with appropriate input from relevant stakeholders? Are decisions being revisited or reversed frequently?
4. **Innovation Rate:** Are people proposing new ideas and taking intelligent risks, or are they playing it safe and avoiding anything that might fail?
5. **Conflict Resolution:** When disagreements arise, are they being resolved constructively, or are they being avoided or escalated unnecessarily?
6. **Feedback Loops:** Are people receiving feedback on their work and decisions? Is that feedback being acted upon?
7. **Cross-Functional Collaboration:** Are teams working effectively across organizational boundaries, or are silos forming?
8. **Leadership Accessibility:** Do people feel they can approach leadership with concerns or ideas? Are leaders aware of problems before they escalate into crises?

Response Protocol:

When trust breakdown indicators are detected:

1. **Immediate Assessment:** Gather data to understand the scope and severity of the trust breakdown. Is it localized to a specific team or relationship, or is it systemic?
2. **Stakeholder Communication:** Communicate with affected parties about what you've observed and what you're doing to address it. Transparency about the process helps rebuild trust.
3. **Root Cause Analysis:** Investigate the underlying causes of the trust breakdown. Was it a specific incident, a pattern of behavior, a system failure, or a combination of factors?
4. **Containment:** Take immediate steps to prevent the trust breakdown from spreading or causing additional damage. This might include clarifying roles and responsibilities, improving communication processes, or addressing specific behavioral issues.
5. **Recovery Planning:** Develop a plan for rebuilding trust, including specific actions, timelines, and success metrics.
6. **System Strengthening:** Identify changes to systems, processes, or policies that could prevent similar trust breakdowns in the future.
7. **Monitoring and Follow-up:** Establish ongoing monitoring to ensure that trust is being rebuilt and that the underlying issues have been resolved.

This systematic approach to trust breakdown mirrors the structured incident response processes that have proven effective in cybersecurity. By treating trust failures as incidents that require investigation, response, and learning, organizations can build more resilient trust systems over time.

The Competitive Advantage of Systems Thinking

Most leadership and organizational development approaches focus either on individual skills or on broad cultural change. Individual-focused approaches assume that if leaders develop better emotional intelligence, communication skills, or decision-making capabilities, trust will naturally follow. Culture-focused approaches assume that if organizations can shift their values, norms, and practices, trust will emerge as a byproduct.

Both approaches have merit, but they overlook the middle layer—the systems and processes that translate individual capabilities and cultural values into day-to-day organizational behavior. This is where the cybersecurity analogy is most potent. Cybersecurity professionals don't just train people to be more security-conscious; they also try to create a "security culture." They design technical and procedural systems that enhance security, detect security issues early, and respond effectively when security is compromised.

The same systems thinking can be applied to trust. Instead of relying on good intentions and cultural values to produce trustworthy behavior, we can design organizational systems that increase the likelihood of trust, detect trust issues early, and recover effectively when trust is compromised (Figure 1.1).

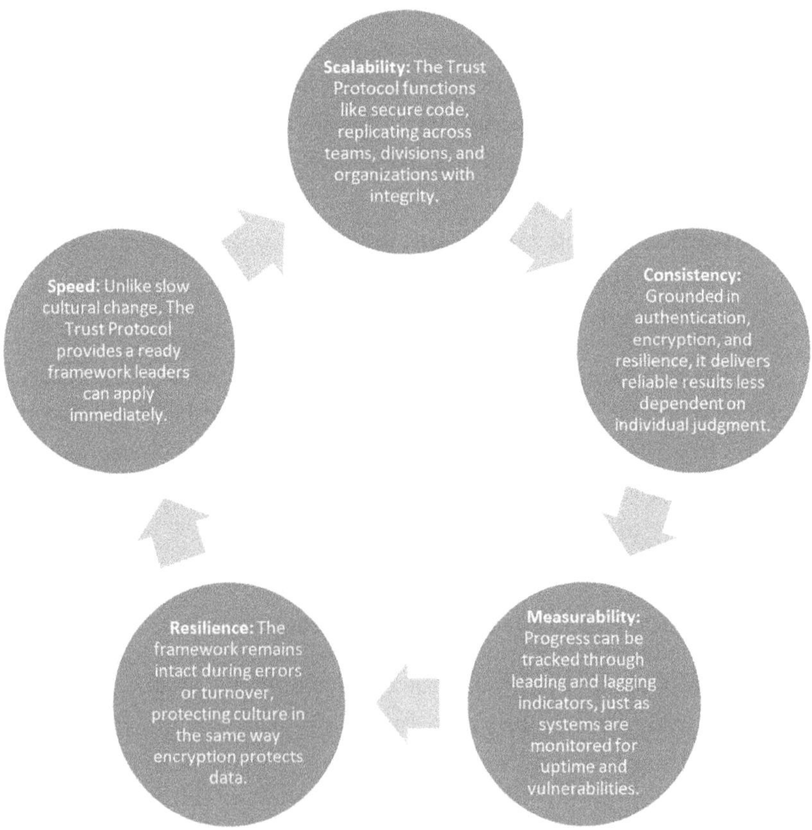

Figure 1.1 Continuous Scaling Model

This systematic approach offers several competitive advantages:

The cybersecurity field has demonstrated the power of this systems approach. Twenty years ago, information security was primarily focused on training individuals to be more cautious and fostering a "security-conscious culture." Today, while training and culture remain essential, the focus has shifted to designing systems that assume people will make mistakes and that provide multiple layers of protection, detection, and response.

Trust systems can evolve in the same direction. Instead of relying primarily on individual trustworthiness and organizational culture, we can build a trust infrastructure that makes trustworthy behavior more likely and mitigates residual risk damage from trust breakdowns.

The Path Forward

The remainder of this book will explore how to build this trust infrastructure using principles and practices adapted from cybersecurity. Each chapter will focus on a specific aspect of trust systems:

- **Authentication:** How leaders can prove their credibility and consistency over time
- **Encryption:** How to create psychological safety that protects vulnerable information and enables honest communication
- **Resilience:** How to plan for and recover from inevitable trust breakdowns
- **Human Firewall:** How to build team-based immunity to trust threats
- **Trust as Code:** How to embed trust into organizational systems and processes
- **Future-Proofing:** How to maintain trust in an age of AI, automation, and algorithmic decision-making

Each chapter will include specific tools, frameworks, and practices that leaders can implement immediately. These aren't abstract concepts or aspirational goals; they're practical systems that can be designed, implemented, monitored, and improved over time.

The goal isn't to eliminate all trust problems; that's neither possible nor desirable. Trust requires vulnerability, and vulnerability always involves risk. The goal is to build systems that increase the likelihood of trust, detect trust issues early, and recover quickly and effectively when trust is compromised.

In cybersecurity, we've learned that perfect security is impossible, but resilient security is achievable. The same is true for trust. Ideal trust is rare, but resilient trust is trust that can withstand stress, recover from damage, and grow stronger over time. Resilient trust makes it possible and essential for organizational success in an increasingly complex and fast-paced world.

The organizations that master this approach will have a significant competitive advantage. They'll make better decisions faster, adapt more quickly to changing conditions, attract and retain better talent, and build stronger relationships with customers, partners, and stakeholders. They'll be more innovative, more resilient, and more successful over the long term.

2

Authentication

Show Me You're Real

In the sterile glow of a security operations center at 3:47 AM, Sarah watched as her team's monitoring systems lit up like a Christmas tree. Red alerts cascaded across multiple screens, each one representing a potential breach attempt. As the Chief Information Security Officer for a Fortune 500 financial services company, she had seen this scenario countless times before. But tonight was different. Tonight, the attack wasn't coming from outside their network; it was coming from within, from a trusted user whose credentials had been compromised.

"Authentication failed," the system announced in its cold, mechanical voice. "Access denied."

In that moment, Sarah realized something profound: the same principles that protected her company's digital assets could revolutionize how leaders establish and maintain trust with their teams. Just as cybersecurity systems continuously verify digital identities, effective leaders must constantly authenticate their credibility through consistent actions, transparent communication, and unwavering integrity under pressure.

This is the essence of leadership authentication, the ongoing process of proving who you are, not just in moments of triumph, but especially when the stakes are highest, and the pressure is most intense. Unlike a simple password that grants one-time access, leadership authentication is a continuous verification process that builds trust incrementally through every interaction, decision, and crisis response.

What Cybersecurity Gets Right about Identity

The cybersecurity industry has spent decades refining the art of identity verification, developing sophisticated frameworks that offer invaluable lessons about authentic leadership. At its core, cybersecurity

DOI: 10.1201/9781003688815-3

authentication operates on three fundamental principles: something you know (knowledge), something you have (possession), and something you are (inherence). When applied to leadership, these same principles create a robust framework for establishing and maintaining authentic authority.

In the digital realm, multi-factor authentication has become the gold standard precisely because it recognizes that no single verification method is foolproof. A password can be stolen, a security token can be lost, but when multiple authentication factors are required simultaneously, the system becomes exponentially more secure. Leadership authentication works the same way. A leader who relies solely on their title, charisma, or past achievements is operating with single-factor authentication and is vulnerable to failure if that one factor is compromised.

Consider the case of Marcus Rodriguez, a newly promoted VP of Operations at a manufacturing company. Marcus had built his reputation on his technical expertise and problem-solving abilities. His "something you know" factor. However, when a major equipment failure threatened to shut down production for weeks, his team discovered that Marcus's knowledge alone wasn't enough. They needed to see evidence of his commitment to their welfare, something you have in this case through a track record of putting people first, and to witness his authentic leadership style under extreme pressure, something you are, as true character is revealed in crisis.

The cybersecurity concept of "zero trust" architecture provides another crucial insight for leadership authentication. In zero-trust systems, no user or device is automatically trusted, regardless of their location or previous access history. Every access request is thoroughly verified, every transaction is carefully authenticated, and every interaction is closely monitored. This might sound paranoid, but it's actually liberating for leaders who embrace this mindset.

Zero trust leadership doesn't mean being suspicious of your team members; it means recognizing that trust must be continuously earned and re-earned through consistent actions. It means understanding that your leadership credentials expire daily and must be renewed through authentic behavior, transparent communication, and reliable follow-through. Just as a security system doesn't take offense when asked to verify credentials for the thousandth time, authentic leaders don't bristle when their team members need ongoing proof of their commitment and competence.

The concept of "least privilege access" in cybersecurity also translates powerfully to leadership contexts. In secure systems, users are granted only the minimum level of access necessary to perform their functions. Similarly, authentic leaders understand that authority should be exercised judiciously, with power distributed appropriately throughout the organization rather than hoarded at the top. This approach not only reduces the risk of abuse but also creates multiple points of authentication throughout the leadership structure.

Digital certificate authorities provide another valuable model for leadership authentication. In cybersecurity, certificate authorities are trusted third parties that verify the identity of entities requesting digital certificates. They conduct rigorous background checks, validate credentials, and issue certificates that other systems can rely on. In leadership contexts, these certificate authorities might be mentors, board members, industry peers, or even team members who can vouch for a leader's authenticity and competence.

The most sophisticated cybersecurity systems also employ behavioral analytics to monitor activity and detect anomalies that might indicate compromised credentials. If a user who typically accesses the system during business hours suddenly logs in at 3 AM from a foreign country, the system flags the login as suspicious and requires additional verification. Leaders can apply the same principle by developing self-awareness of their behavioral patterns and establishing systems to alert them when they're acting inconsistently with their stated values or usual leadership style.

The Cost of Inconsistent Leadership

The financial services industry learned this lesson the hard way during the 2008 financial crisis, when leaders who had built reputations as prudent risk managers were revealed to have been taking enormous gambles with other people's money. The authentication failure wasn't just about competence—it was about the fundamental disconnect between their public personas and their private actions. The cost wasn't just measured in dollars lost, but in trust destroyed, careers ruined, and an entire industry's credibility shattered.

Research conducted by the Harvard Business School found that organizations with inconsistent leadership experience 23% higher employee turnover, 31% lower productivity metrics, and 41% more workplace conflicts than organizations with leaders who consistently demonstrate their values and commitments. These statistics represent real human costs in terms of stress, disengagement, and lost potential.

When leaders are inconsistent between their words and actions, it creates a ripple effect throughout the organization. Team members expend significant mental energy trying to reconcile this mismatch, which not only reduces productivity but also undermines psychological safety and team cohesion. Consistent, authentic leadership is therefore essential to maintaining trust and high-functioning teams.

The technology sector provides numerous examples of authentication failures and their consequences. Consider the case of Elizabeth Holmes and Theranos, where the fundamental authentication failure wasn't just about the technology that didn't work; it was about a leader who consistently presented herself as something she wasn't. The company's board, investors, employees, and customers all suffered because they trusted credentials that were never correctly verified. The authentication system failed at every level, from technical competence to ethical integrity to basic honesty about capabilities and limitations.

But authentication failures don't always involve fraud or deception. Sometimes they're simply the result of leaders who haven't developed robust systems for maintaining consistency under pressure. Take the example of David Kim, a well-respected CEO of a mid-sized software company who prided himself on his collaborative leadership style and commitment to work-life balance. When his company faced a potential acquisition that could save hundreds of jobs, David found himself working 80-hour weeks and making unilateral decisions without consulting his usual advisory groups.

His team understood the pressure he was under. Still, they began to question whether his previous collaborative approach had been authentic or simply a luxury he could afford during easier times. Employee engagement scores dropped 15% during the acquisition period, not because people disagreed with his decisions, but because they encountered authentication failures.

The cost of inconsistent leadership extends beyond immediate organizational impacts. It enables what cybersecurity professionals call "lateral movement." Once trust is compromised in one area, the damage spreads to other areas of the relationship. An employee who loses faith in their leader's commitment to work-life balance may also begin to question their leader's commitment to professional development, fair compensation, or strategic vision. The authentication failure cascades through multiple dimensions of the leadership relationship.

This is why cybersecurity systems don't just lock out users after authentication failures; they also log and analyze them to identify patterns and prevent future breaches. Leaders need similar systems to track and learn from their own authentication failures. When you promise to respond to emails within 24 hours but consistently take 3 days, that's not just a time-management issue; it's an authentication failure that erodes trust in your reliability across all areas of leadership.

The most insidious cost of inconsistent leadership is that it trains team members to become authentication experts themselves, albeit in an unproductive manner. Instead of focusing on their work, they constantly monitor their leader's behavior for signs of inconsistency, mixed messages, or hidden agendas. They develop sophisticated pattern recognition systems to detect when their leader is stressed, distracted, or operating with ulterior motives. This hypervigilance is exhausting and ultimately counterproductive for everyone involved.

"False Logins" in Workplace Behavior

In cybersecurity, a false login occurs when someone uses stolen or compromised credentials to gain unauthorized access to a system. The person appears to be legitimate based on their credentials, but their actual identity and intentions are fraudulent. Workplace behavior is rife with similar false logins. False logins are situations where leaders present themselves as something they're not, often without conscious deception but with equally damaging results.

One of the most common forms of false leadership is what we might call "borrowed authority." When leaders rely on their title, their company's reputation, or their past achievements to authenticate their current competence and commitment. Like using an expired security certificate, this approach may work temporarily, but it inevitably fails under real-world stress testing.

Consider the phenomenon of "meeting theater," where leaders go through the motions of collaborative decision-making while having already decided on a course of action. They facilitate discussions, solicit input, and appear to weigh different options, but their authentication credentials are invalid. They're not actually the collaborative leader they're presenting as. Team members often sense this inauthenticity, even if they can't articulate precisely what feels wrong about the process.

Another standard false login is "empathy simulation," where leaders use the language and gestures of emotional intelligence without genuinely caring for their team members' well-being. They might say all the right things about work-life balance, professional development, and psychological safety, but their actions reveal different priorities. Like a sophisticated phishing attack that perfectly mimics a legitimate website, empathy simulation can be challenging to detect initially, but it eventually reveals itself through inconsistencies and failed follow-through.

The "innovation impostor" represents another type of false login, prevalent in technology and creative industries. These leaders position themselves as forward-thinking disruptors, yet they are actually risk-averse traditionalists. They use the vocabulary of innovation—talking about "failing fast," "thinking outside the box," and "embracing change"—but their actual decision-making patterns reveal a preference for safe, conventional approaches. When their teams propose genuinely innovative ideas that involve real risk or uncertainty, the authentication failure becomes apparent.

"Transparency theater" is perhaps the most damaging form of false leadership in modern times. Leaders who engage in transparency theater selectively share information, creating the appearance of openness while maintaining tight control over what their teams know and when they disclose it. They might hold regular "all-hands" meetings and maintain open-door policies, but the information they share is carefully curated to support predetermined narratives rather than genuinely inform decision-making.

The "servant leadership" false login occurs when leaders adopt the language and superficial behaviors of servant leadership while maintaining fundamentally self-serving motivations. They might talk about "serving their teams" and "removing obstacles." Still, their actions consistently prioritize their own career advancement, recognition, or comfort over the needs and development of their team members.

False logins in workplace behavior are particularly dangerous because they often involve leaders who aren't consciously trying to deceive anyone. They may genuinely believe they embody the qualities they're projecting, making the authentication failure even more challenging to detect and address. Unlike malicious hackers who know they're using stolen credentials, these leaders are often victims of their own self-deception.

The technology industry's concept of "privilege escalation" provides another practical framework for understanding workplace false logins. In cybersecurity, privilege escalation occurs when an attacker gains access to levels of privilege they should not have, often by exploiting vulnerabilities in the authentication system. In leadership contexts, privilege escalation might involve leaders who use their position to access information, make decisions, or influence outcomes beyond their actual area of competence or authority.

For example, a leader might use their technical background to authenticate their opinions on marketing strategy or leverage their success in one division to justify decisions affecting completely different parts of the organization. Like compromised user accounts that suddenly start accessing sensitive databases, these leaders have no business touching them; they are operating outside their legitimate scope of authority, even if they have the formal credentials to do so.

The concept of "session hijacking" also applies to leadership contexts. In cybersecurity, session hijacking occurs when an attacker takes over a legitimate user's authenticated session. In workplace settings, this might manifest as leaders who "hijack" their team's successes, taking credit for achievements they didn't contribute to, or appropriating ideas without acknowledgment. The authentication credentials (their leadership position) are legitimate, but they're using them to claim ownership of assets (achievements, ideas, relationships) that don't belong to them.

The Commitment Audit

Just as cybersecurity professionals conduct regular audits to verify that access controls are functioning correctly and that user credentials haven't been compromised, leaders need systematic approaches to audit their own commitment and consistency. The commitment audit is a structured process for evaluating whether your actions align with your stated values, whether your promises match your performance, and whether your leadership authentication remains strong across different contexts and stress levels.

The first component of a commitment audit involves what cybersecurity professionals call "access logging." Access logging creates a detailed record of your leadership decisions and actions over time. Most leaders have excellent memories for their successes and good intentions, but they often lack systematic data about their actual behavior patterns. A commitment audit requires you to track your actions with the same rigor that security systems track user activity.

This might involve keeping a leadership journal that records not just what you decided, but why you chose it, what factors influenced your thinking, and how your decision aligned with your stated values and commitments. It means tracking your response times to team member requests, monitoring your consistency in applying policies and standards, and documenting how your behavior changes under different types of pressure.

Sarah Martinez, the Chief Technology Officer at a rapidly growing fintech startup, implemented a commitment audit system after realizing that her team's trust in her leadership was eroding despite her best intentions. She began tracking her daily interactions using a simple spreadsheet that recorded her commitments, deadlines, and follow-through rates. Within three months, she discovered patterns she hadn't been aware of: she consistently over-promised during Monday morning meetings when she was feeling optimistic about the week ahead, and she regularly deprioritized one-on-one meetings with team members when project deadlines approached.

The data was uncomfortable but invaluable. Sarah realized that her authentication failures weren't due to bad intentions or a lack of care; they stemmed from predictable patterns in her decision-making that she could address systematically. She began building buffer time into her commitments, scheduling one-on-one meetings during less stressful periods, and developing scripts for communicating when she needed to adjust previously made commitments.

The second component of a commitment audit involves "vulnerability scanning." Vulnerability scanning systematically identifies the conditions under which your leadership authentication is most likely to fail. Just as cybersecurity systems scan for potential weaknesses that attackers could exploit, leaders need to understand their own vulnerability patterns.

Common leadership vulnerabilities include specific types of stress (such as financial pressure, time constraints, and interpersonal conflict), particular personality types or communication styles that trigger defensive responses, and situations where personal interests may conflict with team or organizational needs. The goal isn't to eliminate these vulnerabilities, that's neither possible nor necessary, but to develop awareness and mitigation strategies.

From my experience, putting leaders through high-stakes, simulated situations can surface important behavioral patterns. Do they become controlling under pressure? Avoid tough conversations with top performers? Overcommit to motivate the team? Understanding these tendencies allows leaders to anticipate challenges and implement practical countermeasures that preserve trust, psychological safety, and team cohesion.

These stress tests, however, are only valuable if the results are shared transparently with the individuals involved. Open discussion of the findings gives leaders a clear opportunity to improve and ensures that both managers and employees understand the behaviors being addressed. If this transparency isn't maintained, the process undermines the leadership pillar of authenticity, breeds contempt, and can fracture trust within the team.

The third component involves "credential verification." This is the regular check to ensure your leadership credentials (skills, knowledge, relationships, reputation) remain current and valid. In cybersecurity, credentials have expiration dates and must be renewed periodically. Leadership credentials work similarly, but their expiration dates are often invisible, and the renewal process is less formal.

This might involve seeking 360-degree feedback from team members, peers, and supervisors to verify that your self-perception aligns with others' experiences of your leadership. It could include staying current with industry trends and best practices to ensure your knowledge credentials remain up to date. It might involve regularly reassessing your relationships with key stakeholders to ensure that your influence and credibility haven't been compromised by changing circumstances or competing priorities.

The fourth component of a commitment audit is "incident response planning." Organizations that develop systematic approaches for handling authentication failures when they occur have also embraced incident response planning, which is critical for commitment auditing. In cybersecurity, incident response plans outline exactly what steps to take when a security breach is detected, who should be notified, how to contain the damage, and how to prevent similar incidents in the future. Leaders need similar plans for handling breaches of trust and failures of commitment.

An effective leadership incident response plan includes scripts for acknowledging mistakes quickly and transparently, processes for assessing the scope and impact of the authentication failure, strategies for rebuilding trust with affected team members, and systems for learning from the incident to prevent recurrence. The plan should be developed before it's needed, when emotions are calm, and thinking is clear, rather than in the heat of a crisis when defensive reactions are more likely to compound the original problem.

The final component involves "continuous monitoring. Ensuring ongoing systems for real-time tracking of leadership authentication, rather than relying on periodic audits. This might involve regular check-ins with trusted advisors who can provide honest feedback about your consistency and credibility, automated reminders to review your commitments and deadlines, or simple daily reflection practices that help you stay aware of your alignment between intentions and actions.

Tool: Trust Incident Response Simulator (TIRS)

The Trust Incident Response Simulator (TIRS) represents a breakthrough in leadership development methodology, combining the rigorous scenario-based training used in cybersecurity with the nuanced interpersonal dynamics of organizational leadership. Just as cybersecurity professionals use tabletop exercises and red team simulations to prepare for potential breaches, leaders can use TIRS to rehearse their responses to trust-threatening situations before they occur in real life.

The TIRS framework is built around the recognition that trust failures in leadership rarely happen suddenly; they typically result from a cascade of small authentication failures that compound over time until they reach a crisis point. By simulating these scenarios in a controlled environment, leaders can identify their vulnerability patterns, practice more effective responses, and develop the muscle memory needed to maintain authenticity under pressure.

Core Architecture of TIRS

The TIRS system operates on four foundational principles derived from cybersecurity incident response frameworks: Detection, Analysis, Containment, and Recovery. Each simulated scenario guides participants through all four phases, helping them develop comprehensive skills for managing trust incidents from initial recognition through complete relationship restoration.

Detection Phase: Participants learn to recognize early warning signs of trust erosion, including subtle changes in team communication patterns, decreased engagement in meetings, increased formal documentation of interactions, and shifts in the types of questions team members ask. The simulation presents these warning signs in realistic contexts, helping leaders develop sensitivity to trust-related indicators they might otherwise miss.

Analysis Phase: Once a potential trust incident is detected, participants practice rapid assessment techniques to understand the scope, severity, and root causes of the authentication failure. This involves gathering information from multiple perspectives, identifying which relationships and processes have been affected, and determining whether the incident represents an isolated event or part of a larger pattern.

Containment Phase: The simulation guides participants through strategies for preventing trust damage from spreading to other relationships or areas of responsibility. This might involve direct communication with affected team members, transparent acknowledgment of mistakes, and immediate changes to prevent similar incidents.

Recovery Phase: The final phase focuses on rebuilding trust and implementing systemic changes to prevent recurrence. Participants practice having difficult conversations, making meaningful amends, and demonstrating sustained behavior change over time (Figure 2.1).

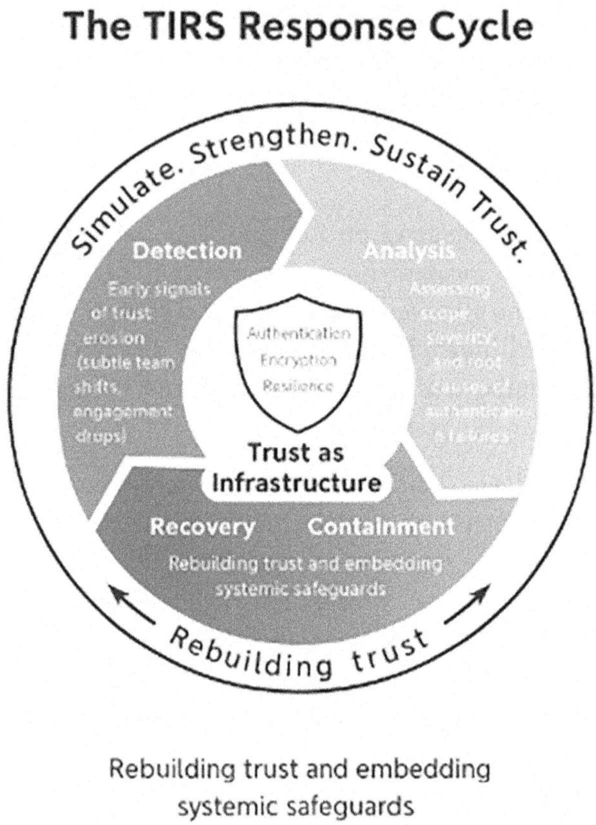

Figure 2.1 TIRS Response Cycle (This image was generated using SORA (AI image-generation tool) in Q4 2025 and selected by the author for conceptual accuracy and analytical clarity).

Role-Based Scripts and Facilitator Guidance

The TIRS system includes detailed, role-based scripts for typical organizational personas, enabling realistic, and multi-perspective simulations. These scripts are based on extensive research into how different personality types, communication styles, and managerial roles respond to incidents involving trust.

The Skeptical Analyst: This role represents team members who are naturally cautious and detail-oriented. They tend to notice inconsistencies quickly and require substantial evidence before rebuilding trust. The script includes typical questions they might ask, concerns they're likely to raise, and the types of reassurance they find most convincing.

The Loyal Supporter: This persona represents team members who have strong positive relationships with the leader and may initially resist acknowledging trust issues. The script examines how these individuals handle authentication failures and what they require to maintain their support while still holding the leader accountable.

The Disengaged Observer: This role describes team members who have already experienced erosion of trust and have psychologically withdrawn from the relationship. The script reflects their tendency to interpret new information through a lens of skepticism and their resistance to re-engagement efforts.

The Anxious Performer: This persona represents high-achieving team members who are particularly sensitive to leadership inconsistency because it threatens their sense of security and predictability. The script includes their tendency to seek frequent reassurance and their need for clear, consistent communication.

The Peer Competitor: This role represents colleagues at the same organizational level who may have mixed motivations regarding the leader's trust incident. The script examines how peer relationships complicate trust recovery efforts and identifies the most effective strategies for maintaining lateral credibility.

Facilitator guidance materials provide detailed instructions for creating psychologically safe simulation environments, managing emotional reactions during intense scenarios, and helping participants extract maximum learning from each exercise. The guidance includes techniques for maintaining appropriate challenge levels—ensuring scenarios are stressful enough to be realistic without being traumatic or counterproductive.

Escalation Cues and Debrief Templates

One of the most sophisticated aspects of TIRS is its dynamic escalation system, which adjusts the scenario's complexity based on participants' responses. If a leader handles initial trust challenges effectively, the simulation introduces additional complications that test their resilience and adaptability. If they struggle with basic authentication failures, the system provides extra support and simpler scenarios to build foundational skills.

Escalation cues are built into each scenario, triggered by specific participant actions or responses. For example, if a leader attempts to deflect responsibility during the Analysis phase, the simulation might introduce a team member who has documented evidence of the leader's inconsistent behavior. If a leader demonstrates genuine accountability and learning, the scenario might fast-forward to test their ability to maintain new behaviors under ongoing pressure.

The debrief templates provide structured frameworks for extracting learning from each simulation experience. These templates guide participants through systematic reflection on their decision-making processes, emotional reactions, and behavioral patterns. They include specific questions designed to help leaders identify their authentication strengths and vulnerabilities, recognize patterns in their responses to different types of trust challenges, and develop personalized action plans for improvement.

Immediate Reaction Debrief: Conducted immediately after each scenario, this template captures participants' emotional responses, initial insights, and areas of confusion or surprise. The questions are designed to help participants process their experience while the details are still fresh and their emotional reactions are still accessible.

Pattern Analysis Debrief: Conducted after multiple scenarios, this template helps participants identify recurring themes in their responses, consistent strengths they can leverage, and persistent vulnerabilities they need to address. The analysis compares their stated values and leadership philosophy to identify areas of alignment and disconnect.

Action Planning Debrief: The final template guides participants in developing specific, measurable commitments to improve their leadership authenticity. These plans include concrete behavioral changes, accountability systems, and methods for tracking progress over time.

Scoring Matrix for Recovery Effectiveness

The TIRS scoring system evaluates leadership performance across multiple dimensions, providing nuanced feedback that goes beyond simple success-or-failure metrics. The matrix is designed to help leaders understand not just what they did right or wrong, but why certain approaches were practical in specific contexts.

Authenticity Score: Measures the consistency between the leader's stated values and their actions during the simulation. This score considers not only what the leader says, but also how they say it, whether their nonverbal communication aligns with their words, and whether their responses come across as genuine to other participants.

Responsiveness Score: Evaluates how quickly and appropriately the leader recognizes and responds to trust-related concerns. This includes their ability to detect early warning signs, their willingness to acknowledge problems when they arise, and their speed in implementing corrective actions.

Transparency Score: Assesses the leader's willingness to share relevant information, acknowledge mistakes, and provide honest explanations for their decisions and actions. The score considers both the completeness of information shared and the appropriateness of the level of detail for different audiences.

Consistency Score: Measures the leader's ability to maintain stable behavior patterns across different scenarios and stress levels. This score tracks whether the leader's responses remain aligned with their stated approach as situations become more challenging or complex.

Learning Agility Score: Evaluates the leader's ability to adapt their approach based on feedback and changing circumstances within the simulation. This includes their willingness to try new strategies, their ability to incorporate input from other participants, and their capacity to modify their behavior in real-time.

Relationship Impact Score: Assesses the effect of the leader's actions on their relationships with different types of team members. This score considers not just immediate reactions, but also the likely long-term implications of the leader's approach for trust and collaboration.

Table 2.1 Dimension Rubrics and Weights

DIMENSION	WEIGHT (%)	1—POOR	2—BELOW	3—ADEQUATE	4—STRONG	5—EXEMPLARY
Authenticity	20	Words contradict actions	Mixed signals, partial admission	Admits fault, actions mostly align	Precise alignment, timely accountability	Actions reinforce values, models integrity
Responsiveness	15	Misses or delays detection	Slow or insufficient response	Timely acknowledgment and corrective action	Quick, appropriate under pressure	Proactive detection, rapid, effective action
Transparency	15	Conceals facts	Limited disclosure	Honest, appropriate explanations	Transparent shares context	Complete clarity builds shared understanding
Consistency	15	Fluctuates widely	Inconsistent under stress	Mostly stable with minor slips	Consistent across contexts	Reliable across contexts and time
Learning Agility	15	Ignores feedback	Slow to adapt, superficial	Adapts based on feedback	Integrates learning quickly	Learns systemically, spreads improvements
Relationship Impact	20	Damages relationships	Short-term harm	Rebuilds gradually	Restores trust with effort	Strengthens credibility, long-term trust

The scoring matrix includes detailed rubrics for each dimension, with specific behavioral indicators for different performance levels. Rather than providing simple numerical scores, the system generates narrative feedback that explains the reasoning behind each assessment and offers specific suggestions for improvement (Tables 2.1 and 2.2).

Table 2.2 Performance Bands

BAND	COMPOSITE %	INTERPRETATION	RECOMMENDED NEXT STEPS
Exemplary	85–100	Model performance, scalable	Capture best practices, mentor others
Strong	70–84	Reliable, minor gaps	Targeted coaching, expand scenario complexity
Needs Development	50–69	Inconsistent recovery	Focused remediation, repeat simulations
High Risk	0–49	Unsafe for team trust	Immediate intervention, intensive coaching

Scoring Scale (1–5):

1 = Critical failure, immediate corrective action required
2 = Below expectations, needs focused remediation
3 = Meets expectations, competent under normal pressure
4 = Strong, reliable under stress, models good practice
5 = Exemplary, consistent, inspires trust and learning

Composite Scoring Method:

1. Each dimension scored 1–5.
2. Weighted score = $\Sigma(\text{score} \times \text{weight}) \div 100$.
3. Composite percentage = $(\text{Weighted score} \div 5) \times 100$.

The system produces not just scores but **narrative feedback**, with raters required to provide written evidence for any score below 3. This ensures that leaders walk away with concrete examples, clear areas for improvement, and a personalized action plan.

Advanced TIRS Applications

As leaders become more proficient with basic TIRS scenarios, the system offers advanced applications that address more complex authentication challenges. These include multi-stakeholder scenarios in which leaders must maintain authenticity with groups with conflicting interests, long-term simulations that test consistency over extended periods, and crisis scenarios in which leaders must make rapid decisions with incomplete information while maintaining team trust.

The system also includes industry-specific scenario libraries that address the unique authentication challenges faced by leaders in different sectors. Healthcare scenarios often focus on maintaining team trust while navigating patient safety incidents, whereas technology scenarios address authentication challenges during rapid scaling or major product failures.

Cultural adaptation modules enable the TIRS system to be tailored for diverse organizational cultures and geographic regions, acknowledging that authentic leadership behaviors vary across different contexts while upholding universal principles of consistency, transparency, and genuine care for team members.

The most advanced TIRS applications integrate with real-world leadership development programs, allowing participants to practice scenarios based on the challenges they face in their organizations. These customized simulations offer immediate practical value while developing general authentication skills that can be applied to other leadership contexts.

Practical Knowledge

Leadership authentication is not a destination but a continuous journey of proving your credibility through consistent actions, transparent communication, and unwavering integrity under pressure. Like the cybersecurity systems that protect our most valuable digital assets, effective leadership requires multiple layers of verification, continuous monitoring, and rapid response to authentication failures.

The lessons from cybersecurity are clear: single-factor authentication is vulnerable, zero trust requires continuous verification, and the cost of authentication failures extends far beyond the immediate incident. Leaders who embrace these principles and implement systematic approaches to maintaining their credibility will build more resilient, trusting, and effective organizations.

The commitment audit process provides a practical framework for maintaining leadership authentication. At the same time, the TIRS offers a powerful tool for developing the skills needed to handle trust challenges effectively. Together, these approaches enable leaders to move beyond hoping they'll remain authentic under pressure to systematically build the capabilities needed to maintain credibility in any situation.

As we move forward in an era of increasing transparency and accountability, the leaders who thrive will be those who understand that authentication is not about perfection, consistency, or honesty, but about the courage to acknowledge and learn from failures when they occur. The cybersecurity industry has learned that the goal is not to prevent all attacks, but to detect them quickly, respond effectively, and recover completely. Leadership authentication operates on the same principles: not perfect consistency, but rapid recognition of failures, transparent response, and genuine commitment to improvement.

The stakes are too high and the opportunities too valuable to leave leadership authentication to chance. By applying rigorous, systematic approaches that have made cybersecurity systems increasingly effective, leaders can build the trust and credibility needed to guide their organizations through an uncertain, rapidly changing world. The question is not whether you will face authentication challenges; it's whether you'll be prepared to handle them with the skill, integrity, and authenticity that your team deserves.

3
Encryption
Protect What Matters

Sarah stared at the email draft on her screen for the third time that morning. The quarterly review meeting was in two hours, and she had discovered a critical flaw in the product launch timeline that would delay everything by six weeks. Her finger hovered over the delete key. Again.

In her previous company, bringing bad news had been career suicide. She'd watched colleagues get publicly reprimanded for raising concerns, only to see "troublemakers" quietly let go during the next round of layoffs. The message had been clear: don't rock the boat, don't be the bearer of bad news, and certainly don't challenge the timeline that leadership has already committed to the board.

But this wasn't her previous company. This was supposed to be different. Her new manager, David, had said all the right things during her interview about "psychological safety" and "open communication." Yet here she sat, paralyzed by the same fear that had silenced her before.

The irony wasn't lost on her. In a world where we encrypt our digital communications to protect sensitive data, we often leave our most vulnerable thoughts and concerns completely exposed. Or worse, we bury them so deeply that they never see the light of day. We've mastered the art of protecting our passwords but forgotten how to protect the psychological space where trust is built, and innovation thrives.

This is the paradox of modern leadership: we demand transparency while punishing honesty, we ask for feedback while shooting the messenger, and we claim to want psychological safety while maintaining cultures that reward conformity and silence dissent. The result is organizations filled with encrypted humans—people who have

DOI: 10.1201/9781003688815-4

learned to hide their true thoughts, concerns, and ideas behind layers of corporate speak and careful positioning.

What Is Emotional Encryption?

Emotional encryption is the psychological equivalent of digital security protocols. Just as we use encryption to protect sensitive data from unauthorized access, emotional encryption creates a secure space where people can share their authentic thoughts, concerns, and ideas without fear of retaliation, judgment, or career damage.

However, unlike the binary nature of digital encryption, in which your data is either protected or it isn't, emotional encryption exists on a spectrum. At one end, you have complete psychological safety where people feel free to take risks, make mistakes, and speak truth to power. At the other end, you have a psychological lockdown where people share nothing of substance, creativity dies, and problems fester in silence until they explode.

Most organizations exist somewhere in the middle, with pockets of safety and danger that shift depending on the leader, the team, and the situation. This inconsistency is perhaps more damaging than consistent psychological danger because it creates confusion and anxiety. People often struggle to know when it's safe to be authentic and when they need to put up their defenses.

Consider the anatomy of a psychologically encrypted conversation. When David finally responded to Sarah's email about the product delay, he didn't immediately jump to solutions or assign blame. Instead, he started with validation: "Thank you for bringing this to my attention. I know this wasn't easy to share." He acknowledged the courage it took to deliver difficult news and created space for a deeper conversation about what had led to the discovery and what could be learned from it.

This response activated what psychologists call the "approach system" in Sarah's brain. This is when the neural networks are associated with curiosity, exploration, and growth. When people feel psychologically safe, their brains literally function differently. The amygdala, responsible for threat detection, calms down, allowing the prefrontal cortex to engage in higher-order thinking, creativity, and problem-solving.

Contrast this with Sarah's previous experience, where delivering bad news activated her "avoidance system." This "avoidance system" refers to the neural network responsible for threat detection and self-preservation. In that environment, her brain was constantly scanning for danger, using precious cognitive resources that could have been directed toward innovation and collaboration.

Neuroscience is clear: psychological safety isn't just a nice-to-have cultural element; it's a prerequisite for peak cognitive performance. When people feel emotionally secure, trusting that their authentic selves will be protected, their brains can focus on the work rather than on survival.

However, emotional encryption isn't just about creating safety; it's also about establishing appropriate boundaries. Just as digital encryption protects sensitive information while allowing authorized access, emotional encryption involves knowing what to share, when to share it, and with whom to share it. It's the difference between vulnerability and oversharing, between transparency and too much information.

From my experience, the most effective leaders know the difference between constructive vulnerability and oversharing. Sharing uncertainties with trusted advisors fosters connection, trust, and learning. By contrast, airing personal struggles to anyone, without regard for context, can create discomfort and erode confidence. Developing what I call "vulnerability intelligence" allows leaders to read the room, choose the right audience, and communicate authentically while preserving professional boundaries.

Breaking Trust through Oversharing and Silence

Trust is a delicate ecosystem that can be disrupted by too much information just as easily as by too little. Leaders often swing between these extremes, either sharing everything in the name of transparency or sharing nothing in the name of professionalism. Both approaches can be equally damaging to the psychological safety that trust requires.

Marcus learned this lesson the hard way during his first year as a department head. Committed to being a "transparent leader," he began sharing his doubts, fears, and frustrations with his team. When the company's financial projections looked shaky, he told his team he was "terrified" about potential layoffs. When he disagreed with a decision from senior leadership, he called it "completely idiotic" in a team meeting. When he was having a difficult conversation with his own boss, he shared the play-by-play with his direct reports.

His intentions were good; he wanted to be authentic and keep his team informed. But the result was chaos. His squad became anxious and distracted, spending more time worrying about the company's stability than focusing on their work. They began to question his judgment and his ability to protect them from organizational turbulence. Paradoxically, his attempt to build trust through radical transparency had the opposite effect.

The problem wasn't that Marcus was sharing information; it was that he was sharing unprocessed emotion and uncertainty without context or boundaries. He was treating his team like a therapy group rather than a professional unit that needed clear direction and confident leadership.

Oversharing breaks trust because it violates the implicit contract between leaders and followers. People look to their leaders for stability, direction, and protection from unnecessary anxiety. When leaders dump their unprocessed fears and frustrations on their teams, they're essentially asking their followers to manage the leader's emotions, creating a reversal of roles that creates confusion and insecurity.

And then there is the opposite extreme of complete silence, which can be equally damaging. When leaders share nothing of their inner experience and maintain a facade of perfect confidence and control, they create a different kind of psychological danger. People begin to feel like they're working for a robot rather than a human being, and they start to question whether their own struggles and uncertainties are acceptable.

Jennifer, a senior executive at a technology company, took pride in her professionalism. She never let her team see her sweat, never admitted uncertainty, and never showed emotion at work. She believed this projected strength and competence. But her squad experienced it as coldness and disconnection. They felt they couldn't bring their own challenges to her because she seemed to have none of her own.

The result was a team that looked competent on the surface but was struggling underneath. People were afraid to admit when they were overwhelmed, confused, or making mistakes. Problems were hidden until they became crises, and innovation suffered because no one wanted to risk looking incompetent in front of their seemingly perfect leader.

Both oversharing and silence create what psychologists call "emotional labor." Emotional labor is the exhausting work of managing not only your own emotions but also others' emotions. When leaders overshare, their teams have to manage the leader's anxiety as well as their own. When leaders are emotionally unavailable, their teams must work harder to decipher what the leader is honestly thinking and feeling.

The solution lies in what we might call "calibrated vulnerability": sharing enough of your human experience to create connection and model authenticity, while maintaining enough boundaries to provide the stability and direction that leadership requires.

This calibration requires developing what emotional intelligence researchers call "emotional granularity": the ability to distinguish among different emotional states and understand their appropriate expression. It's the difference between saying "I'm concerned about this quarter's numbers and want to explore some contingency plans" and "I'm terrified we're all going to lose our jobs."

Both statements might reflect the same underlying anxiety, but they create very different psychological environments. The first invites collaboration and problem-solving; the second creates panic and paralysis.

Calibrated vulnerability also requires an understanding of your audience and their needs. What your peer group needs to hear from you is different from what your direct reports need, which is different from what your boss needs. Emotional encryption involves using different "keys" for other relationships, sharing appropriately based on context and the capacity of the ties to hold what you're sharing.

Psychological Safety Culture

Creating a culture of psychological safety requires more than individual acts of vulnerability or transparency. It requires systematic attention to the environmental factors that either support or undermine people's willingness to take risks, speak up, and bring their whole selves to work.

Many organizations recognize that psychological safety strengthens how teams communicate, learn, and respond to challenges. Over time, teams tend to move through recognizable patterns as trust deepens. Teams could start with fundamental inclusion and progress toward more open idea-sharing and constructive dissent. Understanding where a team sits along this continuum helps leaders choose interventions that strengthen confidence, clarity, and participation.

Stage 1: Inclusion Safety is the most basic level, where people feel safe to be themselves and are accepted for who they are. This isn't about agreeing with everyone or avoiding difficult conversations. It's about creating an environment where people's fundamental humanity is respected, regardless of their background, perspective, or role in the organization.

Many organizations struggle even at this basic level. Subtle forms of exclusion can undermine inclusion and safety before more advanced forms of psychological safety can develop. Examples of this include inside jokes that exclude some people, informal networks that bypass certain team members, or communication styles that favor specific personality types.

Building inclusion safety requires leaders to pay attention to the small moments that either welcome people in or push them out. It's about noticing who speaks in meetings and who doesn't, whose ideas get built upon and whose get ignored, who gets invited to informal gatherings and who gets left out. It's about creating multiple pathways for participation and recognizing that not everyone contributes in the same way.

Stage 2: Learner Safety emerges when people feel secure enough to engage in the learning process; to ask questions, make mistakes, and acknowledge what they don't know. This is where curiosity can flourish and where people can take the intellectual risks necessary for growth and innovation.

Learner safety is often undermined by cultures that punish questions as signs of incompetence or that treat mistakes as character flaws rather than learning opportunities. When people are afraid to admit what they don't know, they stop asking for help, stop experimenting, and stop growing.

Creating learner safety requires leaders to model their own learning process. Ask questions publicly, admit when you don't know something, and celebrate intelligent failures. It requires creating formal and informal opportunities for people to experiment, learn, and share what they've discovered.

Stage 3: Contributor Safety develops when people feel safe to contribute their unique skills, perspectives, and ideas to the team's work. This is where diversity of thought becomes a competitive advantage rather than a source of conflict.

Contributor safety is often hindered by hierarchical cultures that prioritize input from only certain levels or functional areas, or by group dynamics that favor conformity over creativity. When people feel like their contributions aren't valued or that speaking up will be seen as overstepping their role, they withdraw their discretionary effort and creativity.

Building contributor safety requires leaders to actively seek out diverse perspectives, create structured opportunities for input from all levels of the organization, and demonstrate that they value substance over status. It requires moving beyond the rhetoric of "we value everyone's input" to create systems and processes that actually make space for that input.

Stage 4: Challenger Safety is the highest level, where people feel safe challenging the status quo, questioning decisions, and speaking truth to power. This is where breakthrough innovation happens and where organizations can avoid the groupthink that leads to catastrophic failures.

Challenger safety is the most difficult to achieve because it requires leaders to welcome dissent and disagreement, even when it's uncomfortable or inconvenient. It requires creating channels for people to raise concerns without fear of retaliation and demonstrating that challenging ideas and challenging people are two different things.

The most psychologically safe organizations don't just tolerate challenger safety; they actively cultivate it. They conduct "red team" exercises in which people are specifically asked to find flaws in plans. They rotate devil's advocate roles in meetings. They celebrate the people who raise difficult questions and challenge assumptions, even when those challenges are ultimately proven wrong.

But psychological safety culture isn't just about these four stages; it's also about the systems and structures that either support or undermine safety over time. It's about hiring practices that prioritize cultural fit alongside technical skills. It's about performance management systems that reward collaboration and learning, not just individual achievement. It's about meeting structures that create space for all voices, not just the loudest ones.

Most importantly, a psychological safety culture requires what researchers call "institutional memory." This is the ability to maintain safety norms even as people come and go. This means embedding safety practices into the organization's DNA rather than relying on individual leaders to create and support them.

Boundary-Setting for Leaders

One of the most challenging aspects of creating psychological safety is learning to set appropriate boundaries for yourself and your team. Boundaries aren't walls that keep people out; they're containers that create safety for everyone involved.

The paradox of leadership boundaries is that they must be both firm and permeable. Firm enough to create predictability and safety, porous enough to allow for authentic connection and collaboration. Too rigid, and you create distance and formality that inhibits trust. Too loose, and you create chaos and confusion that undermines confidence.

Consider the challenge that Elena faced as a newly promoted team leader. Her previous role as a peer had involved close friendships with several team members; they had shared personal struggles, socialized outside of work, and supported each other through difficult times. Now, as their manager, she needed to maintain those relationships while also giving difficult feedback, making tough decisions about assignments and promotions, and representing the team's interests to senior leadership.

The temptation was to either maintain the same relationship (which would compromise her ability to lead effectively) or to completely shut down personal connections (which would feel like a betrayal to her former peers). Neither extreme would work.

Instead, Elena had to learn what psychologists call "differentiated intimacy"—the ability to maintain close, caring relationships while also maintaining appropriate professional boundaries. This meant having explicit conversations with her team about how their relationships would need to evolve, which conversations were still suitable, and how they would handle situations where her role as a manager might conflict with her role as a friend.

She established what she called "context switching"; clear signals indicating when they were interacting as friends versus in their professional roles. During one-on-one meetings and team meetings, she was their manager first. During informal conversations and social events, she could be their friend first, while still maintaining awareness of her leadership responsibilities.

This kind of boundary-setting requires what researchers call "emotional intelligence" and "social intelligence": the ability to read situations, understand how your behavior affects others, and adjust your approach accordingly. It's not about following rigid rules but about developing the sensitivity to navigate complex relational dynamics.

For leaders, boundary-setting also involves managing what psychologists call "emotional contagion"—the tendency for emotions to spread from person to person, especially from leaders to followers. Research shows that leaders' emotions have a disproportionate impact on their teams' emotional states, productivity, and decision-making.

This means leaders have a responsibility to manage their own emotional state, not just for their own well-being but also for their team's. It doesn't mean being emotionally flat or inauthentic. This means being intentional about how and when you share your emotional experience.

David, the manager who responded so well to Sarah's email about the product delay, had learned this lesson through experience. Early in his leadership career, he had let his stress and frustration show freely, believing that transparency meant sharing everything. But he noticed that his team's energy and confidence seemed to mirror his own emotional state. When he was anxious, they became uneasy. When he was frustrated, they became defensive.

He began to develop what he called "emotional leadership," the practice of managing his own emotional state in service of his team. This didn't mean suppressing his emotions or being inauthentic. It meant processing his emotions privately or with appropriate confidants (his own manager, his spouse, his executive coach) before bringing a more regulated version of himself to his team interactions.

When he felt overwhelmed, he would take time to identify what specifically was causing it and what support he needed. Then he could share with his team in a way that was informative rather than anxiety-provoking: "I'm feeling stretched thin with everything on our plate right now, so I'm going to be asking for more help with prioritization and delegation."

This kind of emotional boundary-setting creates what psychologists call "containment": the ability to hold difficult emotions and experiences without being overwhelmed by them or overwhelming others. It's like being a shock absorber for your team, absorbing some of the organizational turbulence so they can focus on their work.

But boundaries aren't just about managing downward, they're also about managing upward and laterally. Leaders need to set boundaries with their own managers, peer leaders, and other stakeholders who might make unreasonable demands on their time, attention, or the team's resources.

This requires developing the "broken record" skills that assertiveness training calls for. The ability to calmly and consistently maintain your boundaries, even when others push back, requires development. It also requires understanding the difference between being accommodated (adjusting your approach to meeting others' legitimate needs) and being compliant (saying yes to everything to avoid conflict).

The most effective leaders learn to set boundaries proactively rather than reactively. They communicate their team's capacity and constraints before they become overwhelmed. They establish clear expectations about response times, meeting schedules, and availability. They create systems and processes that protect their team's time and energy for high-value work.

Tools: Vulnerability Map and Encrypted Communication Framework

Creating psychological safety requires more than good intentions; it necessitates practical tools and frameworks that can be consistently applied across various situations and relationships. The two tools outlined here provide structured approaches to building and maintaining emotional encryption in your leadership practice.

The Vulnerability Map

The Vulnerability Map is a diagnostic tool that helps leaders assess the current state of psychological safety in their relationships and teams,

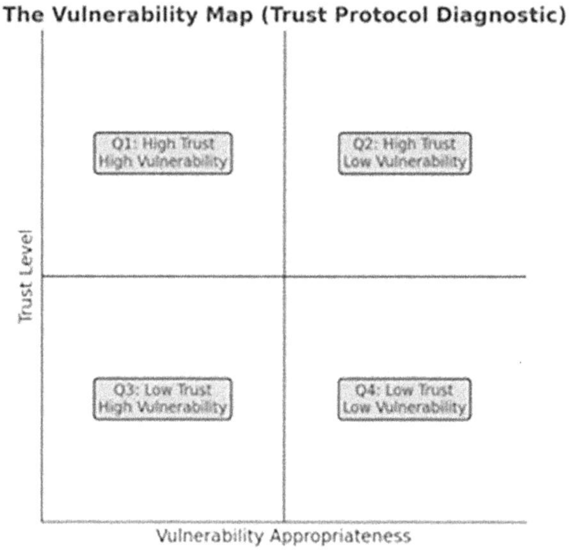

Figure 3.1 The Vulnerability Map. (This image was generated using SORA (AI image-generation tool) in Q4 2025 and selected by the author for conceptual accuracy and analytical clarity).

identify areas for improvement, and track progress over time. It's based on the principle that vulnerability and trust exist on a spectrum and that different relationships require different levels of openness and sharing.

The map consists of four quadrants that represent different combinations of trust level and vulnerability appropriateness (Figure 3.1).

Quadrant 1: High Trust, High Vulnerability Appropriateness

These are your closest professional relationships, trusted advisors, mentors, and perhaps a few peer leaders or direct reports with whom you've built deep mutual trust over time. In these relationships, you can share your deepest concerns, uncertainties, and struggles because you know the other person has both the emotional capacity to hold what you're sharing and the discretion to handle it appropriately.

For Sarah, this might include her mentor from her previous company, her executive coach, and perhaps one or two trusted colleagues who have demonstrated their reliability and wisdom over time. These are the people she can call when she's facing a difficult decision, feeling overwhelmed, or questioning her own judgment.

Quadrant 2: High Trust, Low Vulnerability Appropriateness

These are relationships where you have significant trust but where high levels of vulnerability wouldn't be appropriate due to role differences, power dynamics, or the other person's capacity. This might include your direct reports (where your vulnerability needs to be calibrated to provide stability rather than create anxiety), your boss (where some vulnerability builds connection, but too much might undermine confidence), or newer team members who haven't yet earned the right to hear your deepest concerns.

In these relationships, you might share challenges and uncertainties, but in a way that demonstrates thoughtfulness and leadership rather than creating burden or anxiety. You might say, "I'm working through some complex strategic questions and would value your perspective on this specific aspect" rather than "I have no idea what we should do, and I'm terrified we're making the wrong decision."

Quadrant 3: Low Trust, High Vulnerability Appropriateness

These are relationships where vulnerability might be appropriate given the role or context, but where trust hasn't yet been established. This might include new team members, colleagues from other departments, or external partners where some level of openness is expected but where you don't yet know how they'll handle what you share.

In these relationships, you might start with small acts of vulnerability. Admitting when you don't know something, sharing a minor struggle or uncertainty, or asking for help with a specific challenge. You're essentially testing the waters to see how the other person responds and whether they demonstrate the reliability and discretion needed for deeper sharing over time.

Quadrant 4: Low Trust, Low Vulnerability Appropriateness

These are relationships in which both trust and vulnerability are inappropriate. This might include difficult colleagues, toxic team members, or external stakeholders who have demonstrated that they can't be trusted with sensitive information. In these relationships, you maintain professional courtesy and effectiveness while protecting yourself from potential harm.

This doesn't mean being cold or distant—it means being strategic about what you share and how you share it. You might focus on facts rather than feelings, solutions rather than problems, and outcomes rather than process.

To use the Vulnerability Map effectively, start by listing the key relationships in your professional life and placing each one in the appropriate quadrant. Then ask yourself:

- Are there relationships in Quadrant 1 where you're not taking advantage of the trust and safety that exists? Are you under-sharing in ways that might be limiting your effectiveness or well-being?
- Are there relationships in Quadrant 2 where you might be over-sharing or under-sharing? How can you calibrate your vulnerability to be appropriate for the relationship and context?
- Are there relationships in Quadrant 3 where you could take small steps to build trust and test the waters for greater openness?
- Are there relationships in Quadrant 4 where you need to strengthen your boundaries or develop better strategies for protecting yourself?

The map should be revisited regularly because relationships evolve. Someone who starts in Quadrant 3 might move to Quadrant 2 or even Quadrant 1 as trust develops. Conversely, someone who was in Quadrant 1 might need to be moved to a different quadrant if they violate your trust or demonstrate that they can't handle what you're sharing.

The Encrypted Communication Framework

The Encrypted Communication Framework provides a structured approach to sharing complex, sensitive, or vulnerable information in ways that build trust rather than create anxiety or confusion. It's based on the principle that how you share information is often more important than what you share.

The framework consists of five components that should be present in any high-stakes communication:

1. **Context Setting**

   Before sharing sensitive information, establish the context for why you're sharing it, what you hope to accomplish, and what kind of response you're looking for. This helps the other person understand how to receive and respond to what you're about to share.

For example: "I want to share something with you that I've been struggling with because I value your perspective and think you might have insights that could help me think through this more clearly. I'm not looking for you to solve this for me, but I would appreciate your thoughts on how I might approach it."

2. **Emotional Labeling**

   Clearly identify the emotions you're experiencing rather than expecting the other person to guess or interpret them. This reduces ambiguity and helps the other person respond appropriately.

   For example: "I'm feeling anxious about this decision because there are significant risks either way, and I'm worried about the impact on the team" rather than "This situation is tough" (which could mean anything from mildly challenging to completely overwhelming).

3. **Fact-Feeling Separation**

   Distinguish between objective facts and your subjective interpretation or emotional response to those facts. This helps the other person understand what's actually happening, rather than how you're experiencing it.

   For example: "The client has asked for a 30% reduction in timeline [fact], and I'm concerned that this will compromise quality and put unrealistic pressure on the team [feeling/interpretation]."

4. **Boundary Clarification**

   Be explicit about the kind of support you're seeking and the boundaries for the information you're sharing. This prevents misunderstandings and helps the other person respond in a way that is actually helpful.

   For example: "I'd appreciate your thoughts on this, but I want to be clear that this conversation should stay between us until I've had a chance to think through next steps" or "I'm hoping you can help me brainstorm some options, and then I'll take it from there."

5. **Follow-up Commitment**

   Establish clear expectations about what will happen next and when you'll reevaluate. This creates closure and prevents the other person from worrying about unresolved issues.

For example: "I'm going to think about what you've shared and talk to one other person about this, and then I'll get back to you by Friday with my thoughts on how to move forward."

When Sarah finally sent that email about the product delay, she unconsciously used several elements of this framework:

Context Setting: "I wanted to bring this to your attention as soon as possible because I know it affects our commitments to the board."

Emotional Labeling: "I'm concerned about the implications and want to make sure we're thinking through all the options."

Fact-Feeling Separation: "Based on my analysis of the technical requirements [fact], I believe we need an additional six weeks [fact]. I'm worried about how this will be received [feeling], but think it's better to surface this now rather than later [interpretation]."

Boundary Clarification: "I wanted to give you a heads up before the meeting so you could decide how you want to handle this with the broader team."

Follow-up Commitment: "I'm happy to walk through the details with you and discuss potential alternatives."

The framework can be adapted for different situations and relationships. In a Quadrant 1 relationship, you might spend more time on emotional labeling and less on boundary clarification because the trust level allows for more open sharing. In a Quadrant 4 relationship, you might focus heavily on fact-feeling separation and boundary clarification while minimizing emotional labeling.

The key is to be intentional about each component rather than hoping that the other person will intuitively understand what you need or how to respond. By providing this structure, you're essentially creating the encryption key that allows the other person to safely receive and react to what you're sharing.

As Sarah walked into the quarterly review meeting that afternoon, she felt something she hadn't experienced in years: the confidence that comes from knowing you've done the right thing, even when it's difficult. David not only received her news about the delay with grace and appreciation but also used it as an opportunity to model for the broader team how to handle unexpected challenges.

"Sarah discovered an issue that's going to require us to adjust our timeline," he announced to the group. "I want to start by thanking her for bringing this to our attention early enough that we can address it thoughtfully rather than reactively. This is exactly the kind of proactive problem-solving that makes our team stronger."

The room didn't erupt in panic or finger-pointing. Instead, it shifted into collaborative problem-solving mode. People asked clarifying questions, offered alternative approaches, and began working together to minimize the impact of the delay. Sarah realized she was witnessing something rare: a team that had learned to treat problems as shared challenges rather than individual failures.

This is what emotional encryption makes possible, not the absence of difficult conversations or challenging situations, but the presence of safety that allows people to navigate those challenges together. When people trust that their vulnerability will be protected, know that speaking up will be met with curiosity rather than punishment, and feel confident that their authentic selves are welcome, they can focus their energy on solving problems rather than protecting themselves.

The next chapter will explore how to maintain this kind of psychological safety over time, especially when facing inevitable conflicts and disagreements in any dynamic organization. Because trust isn't just built in moments of vulnerability; it's tested and strengthened in moments of tension.

4

Resilience

Trust Will Break. Prepare for It

> Trust is the confident reliance on the integrity, ability, and character of a person or system.

This definition isn't just philosophical; it's operational. When we break it down, we see that trust rests on three pillars: integrity (doing what you say you'll do), ability (competence to deliver), and character (maintaining consistent values under pressure). But here's what most leadership books won't tell you: these pillars don't just erode gradually over time. They can shatter in an instant, and when they do, the psychological safety you've worked so hard to build can collapse like a house of cards.

The uncomfortable truth is that trust will break. Not might break, will break. In any dynamic organization where real work gets done, where difficult decisions must be made, and where human beings with different perspectives, priorities, and pressures interact daily, trust breaches are not anomalies to be avoided but inevitabilities to be prepared for.

This chapter isn't about preventing trust from breaking; that's a fool's errand. Instead, it's about building organizational resilience that can withstand these inevitable fractures and emerge stronger. We'll explore how to maintain psychological safety not just in the comfortable moments of shared vulnerability, but in the crucible of conflict, disagreement, and yes, broken trust.

The Myth of Unbreakable Trust

Most leadership literature treats trust like a precious vase, something to be carefully protected, never dropped, always handled with white gloves. This metaphor is not only wrong; it's dangerous. It creates leaders who are so afraid of damaging trust that they avoid the very conflicts and difficult conversations that could strengthen it.

DOI: 10.1201/9781003688815-5

Trust isn't a vase. It's more like a muscle. And like any muscle, it grows stronger when it's stressed, tested, and allowed to recover properly. The organizations with the deepest, most resilient trust aren't those that have never experienced conflict; they're the ones that have learned to navigate conflict in ways that deepen relationships rather than damage them.

Consider the TIRS model we've been building throughout this book:

Trust forms the foundation, and it's not static. It's dynamic, constantly being tested and renewed.

Integrity provides the framework, and integrity isn't just about keeping promises when it's easy. It's about maintaining your values when it's hard.

Resilience is what we're focusing on now, the ability to bounce back from trust breaches stronger than before.

Safety is the outcome, and proper psychological safety isn't the absence of conflict. It's the confidence that conflict can be navigated without destroying relationships.

The leaders who understand this create what I call "antifragile trust"; trust that doesn't just survive stress but grows stronger because of it. They don't just build psychological safety; they build psychological resilience (Figure 4.1).

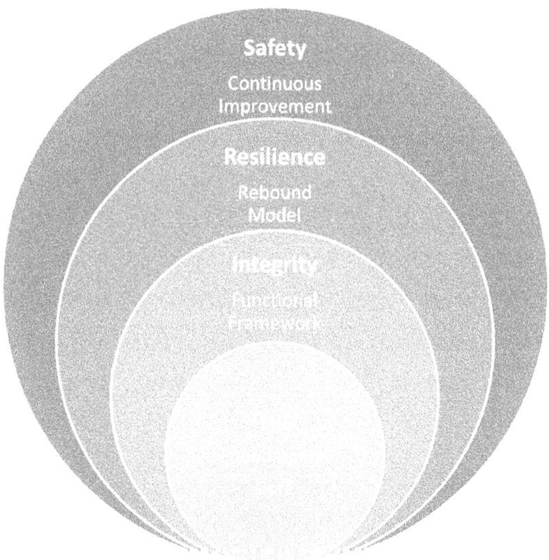

Figure 4.1 TIRS Application Framework.

Planning for the Inevitable Trust Breakdown

In cybersecurity, we have a saying: "It's not if you'll be breached, it's when." The same principle applies to organizational trust. The question isn't whether trust will be broken in your organization; it's whether you'll be ready when it happens.

This requires a fundamental shift in mindset. Instead of viewing trust breaches as failures to be avoided at all costs, we should see them as inevitable events to be prepared for. This doesn't mean we become cavalier about trust or stop working to maintain it. It means we build systems and develop capabilities that allow us to respond effectively when trust is damaged.

The first step is to understand the anatomy of a trust breakdown. Trust doesn't usually shatter all at once; it typically follows a predictable pattern:

The Trigger Event: Something happens that calls into question one of the three pillars of trust: integrity, ability, or character. This could be a missed deadline, a broken promise, a decision that seems to contradict stated values, or a competency gap that becomes apparent under pressure.

The Interpretation Phase: People try to make sense of what happened. This is where the real damage often occurs, not in the original event but in how it's interpreted and communicated (or miscommunicated) throughout the organization.

The Response Window: There's a critical period immediately after the trigger event during which the response can either contain the damage or amplify it exponentially. This window is usually much shorter than leaders realize.

The Ripple Effect: Trust breaches rarely stay contained. They spread through networks of relationships, often growing and distorting as they travel.

The Recovery Phase: This is where most organizations fail. They either ignore the breach, hoping it will go away, or they respond in ways that actually make the situation worse (Figure 4.2).

Understanding this pattern allows us to build intervention points at each stage. However, first, we need to acknowledge that this pattern

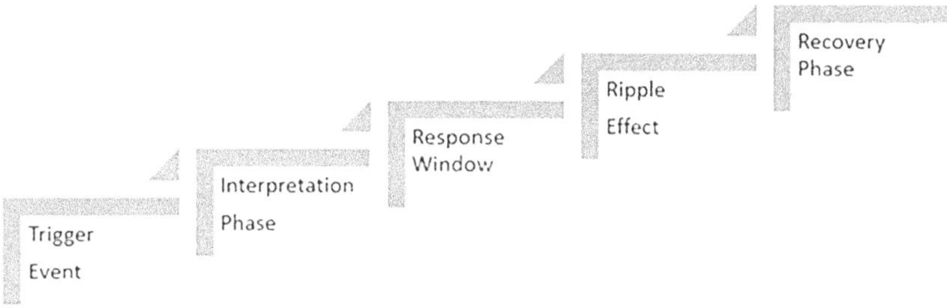

Figure 4.2 Trust recovery workflow.

will likely occur. The organizations that handle trust breaches best aren't those with the fewest breaches—they're those with the best breach response protocols.

Recovery as a System, Not a Reaction

When trust breaks down, most leaders react emotionally. They become defensive, make excuses, try to minimize the damage, or overcorrect in ways that create new problems. This reactive approach is understandable but ineffective. What's needed instead is a systematic approach to trust recovery—one that's planned, practiced regularly, and executed with the same discipline we bring to any other critical organizational capability.

Consider how mature organizations respond to other types of crises. They don't wait for a fire to figure out evacuation procedures. They don't wait for a data breach to occur before developing incident response protocols. They plan, they practice, they refine. The same systematic approach needs to be applied to trust recovery.

A systematic approach to trust recovery has several key components:

Early Detection Systems: Just as we have monitoring systems to detect technical problems before they become critical, we need systems to detect trust erosion before it becomes a complete breach. This means creating multiple channels for feedback, establishing regular trust audits, and training leaders to recognize the early warning signs of trust degradation.

Rapid Response Protocols: When a trust breach occurs, speed matters. The longer the delay between the breach and the response, the greater the damage. This requires pre-established protocols that can be activated quickly, clear roles and responsibilities for who does what, and decision-making frameworks that don't require lengthy deliberation.

Stakeholder Communication Plans: Trust breaches create information vacuums, which are filled with speculation, rumors, and worst-case assumptions. Effective trust recovery requires proactive, transparent communication with all affected stakeholders. This communication needs to be honest about what happened, clear about what's being done to address it, and realistic about timelines for resolution.

Root Cause Analysis: Just as we conduct post-incident reviews for technical failures, we need to conduct thorough analyses of trust breaches. What were the contributing factors? What systemic issues made the breach possible? What can be changed to prevent similar violations in the future? This analysis needs to go beyond individual blame to examine organizational systems, processes, and cultures.

Systematic Rebuilding: Trust recovery isn't just about fixing what broke; it's about rebuilding stronger than before. This requires a systematic approach to demonstrating renewed integrity, ability, and character over time. It's not enough to apologize and promise to do better. There needs to be visible, measurable evidence of change.

The TIRS model provides a framework for this systematic approach. When trust breaks down, we need to:

- **Trust:** Acknowledge the breach honestly and take full responsibility
- **Integrity:** Demonstrate through actions, not just words, that we're committed to doing better
- **Resilience:** Show that we can learn from failure and emerge stronger
- **Safety:** Rebuild the psychological safety that allows people to trust again

This isn't a linear process. These elements need to be addressed simultaneously and continuously throughout the recovery process.

How to Bounce Back with Credibility

Credibility after a trust breach isn't rebuilt through grand gestures or eloquent apologies. It's rebuilt through consistent, small actions over time that demonstrate genuine change. The leaders who successfully recover from trust breaches understand that credibility is earned in drops and lost in buckets, but it can be earned back if you're willing to do the patient, unglamorous work of proving yourself again.

The first principle of credible recovery is radical ownership. This means taking full responsibility for what happened, without excuses, blame-shifting, or minimizing the impact. It means acknowledging not just the immediate breach but the systemic factors that made it possible. Most importantly, it means owning the emotional impact on others, not just the operational consequences.

Radical ownership sounds simple, but it's actually quite difficult for most leaders. Our natural tendency when trust is broken is to protect ourselves, to explain the circumstances, to point out mitigating factors, to share the blame with others. These defensive responses are understandable, but they're also counterproductive. They signal that we're more concerned with protecting our reputation than with addressing the harm we've caused.

Actual radical ownership requires what I call "vulnerable accountability." This means being willing to be seen as fallible, to admit mistakes publicly, and to accept the consequences of those mistakes without trying to negotiate them away. It means saying things like:

"I committed to you that I didn't keep, and I understand that this has damaged your trust in me."
"I realize now that my decision to move forward without consulting the team violated the collaborative values I said were important to me."
"I can see how my actions created doubt about whether I really have the competence to lead this initiative."

These statements are uncomfortable to make, but they're necessary for credible recovery. They demonstrate that you understand the real impact of your actions and that you're not trying to minimize or deflect responsibility.

The second principle of credible recovery is transparent process improvement. It's not enough to acknowledge what went wrong; you need to show specifically what you're doing to prevent it from happening again. This means sharing your analysis of the cause of the breach, outlining the changes you're making to your systems and processes, and providing regular updates on your progress.

This transparency serves multiple purposes. First, it demonstrates that you're taking the breach seriously and investing real effort in preventing recurrence. Second, it allows others to provide input and feedback on your improvement efforts. Third, it creates accountability. When you've publicly committed to specific changes, people can hold you accountable for following through.

The third principle is patient consistency. Trust recovery doesn't happen on your timeline; it occurs on the timeline of those who were hurt. This means being prepared for a long process of proving yourself through consistent actions over time. It means accepting that people may be skeptical of your efforts initially and that you'll need to demonstrate change repeatedly before it's fully believed.

This patience is perhaps the most challenging part of trust recovery for most leaders. We want to fix things quickly, to move past the uncomfortable period of damaged relationships, to get back to normal. But there is no shortcut through the trust recovery process. The only way out is through, and "through" takes time.

The fourth principle is systemic change, not just personal change. Suppose systemic issues caused the trust breach: poor communication processes, unclear decision-making authority, inadequate resources, conflicting priorities, then personal apologies and promises aren't enough. The systems themselves need to change.

This is where many trust recovery efforts fail. Leaders focus on changing their own behavior but don't address the organizational factors that contributed to the breach. As a result, similar breaches recur, often involving different people, and trust erodes even further.

Systemic change requires looking beyond individual actions to examine organizational structures, processes, and cultures. It means asking questions like:

- What organizational pressures contributed to this breach?
- What systems or processes made this breach more likely?

- What cultural norms or expectations need to change?
- What resources or support were missing that could have prevented this?
- How can we redesign our systems to make similar breaches less likely in the future?

The TIRS model helps guide this systemic analysis:

Trust: What organizational factors make it harder for people to rely on each other?
Integrity: What systemic pressures make it difficult for people to keep their commitments?
Resilience: What organizational capabilities do we need to better handle stress and conflict?
Safety: What structural changes would make people feel safer to speak up about problems before they become crises?

Building the Trust Breach Playbook

Every organization needs a trust breach playbook, a documented set of procedures for responding to trust breakdowns when they occur. This playbook shouldn't be a theoretical document that sits on a shelf; it should be a practical tool that can be activated quickly and executed effectively under pressure.

The trust breach playbook should include several key components:

Breach Classification System: Not all trust breaches are the same. Some are minor misunderstandings that can be resolved quickly with direct conversation. Others are major violations that require extensive recovery efforts. The playbook should include a classification system that helps leaders rapidly assess the severity of a breach and determine the appropriate response level.

A simple classification system might include:

- **Level 1—Minor Breach:** Isolated incident affecting a small number of people, no pattern of similar issues, low impact on operations or relationships
- **Level 2—Moderate Breach:** Affects multiple people or key relationships, may indicate systemic issues, moderate impact on team effectiveness

- **Level 3—Major Breach:** Widespread impact, clear pattern of problems, significant damage to relationships or organizational effectiveness
- **Level 4—Critical Breach:** Threatens organizational survival, involves legal or ethical violations, requires immediate executive intervention

Each level should have corresponding response protocols, escalation procedures, and recovery timelines.

Immediate Response Protocols: The first 24–48 hours after a trust breach are critical. The playbook should include step-by-step procedures for this immediate response period:

- **Assess and Contain:** Quickly assess the scope and impact of the breach. Take immediate steps to prevent further damage.
- **Notify Key Stakeholders:** Inform relevant leaders, team members, and other stakeholders about the breach and the initial response.
- **Gather Information:** Collect facts about what happened, when, and who was affected. Avoid making assumptions or jumping to conclusions.
- **Provide Initial Communication:** Acknowledge that something has happened and that you're taking it seriously. Don't wait until you have all the answers before beginning to communicate.
- **Activate Recovery Team:** Assemble the people who will be responsible for managing the recovery process.

Stakeholder Analysis and Communication Templates: Different stakeholders will be affected differently by trust breaches and will need different types of communication. The playbook should include templates for communicating with:

- **Direct Reports:** Team members who work closely with the person whose trust was breached
- **Peers:** Other leaders at the same organizational level
- **Senior Leadership:** Executives who need to be informed about significant trust issues
- **Customers or External Partners:** When trust breaches affect external relationships
- **Broader Organization:** When trust breaches have organization-wide implications

Each template should be customizable but include key elements such as acknowledgment of the breach, explanation of immediate actions being taken, a timeline for further communication, and contact information for questions.

Recovery Planning Framework: The playbook should include a structured approach to developing recovery plans. This framework should address:

- **Root Cause Analysis:** A Systematic process for understanding what caused the breach
- **Stakeholder Impact Assessment:** Analysis of how different groups were affected
- **Recovery Objectives:** Clear, measurable goals for the recovery process
- **Action Planning:** Specific steps to be taken, with owners and timelines
- **Progress Monitoring:** How recovery progress will be measured and communicated
- **Success Criteria:** How you'll know when trust has been sufficiently rebuilt

Escalation Procedures: The playbook should clearly define when and how to escalate trust breaches to higher levels of leadership. This includes:

- **Escalation Triggers:** Specific criteria that require escalation
- **Escalation Pathways:** Who to contact and in what order
- **Information Requirements:** What information needs to be provided when escalating
- **Decision Authority:** Who has the authority to make different types of decisions during recovery

Recovery Monitoring and Measurement: Trust recovery is not a one-time event but an ongoing process. The playbook should include methods for monitoring progress and measuring success:

- **Trust Surveys:** Regular pulse surveys to measure trust levels over time
- **Behavioral Indicators:** Observable behaviors that indicate trust is being rebuilt
- **Milestone Reviews:** Regular check-ins to assess recovery progress

- **Feedback Mechanisms:** Ways for stakeholders to provide ongoing feedback about recovery efforts

The TIRS model provides a valuable framework for organizing the playbook:

Trust Section: Procedures for acknowledging breaches and taking responsibility
Integrity Section: Guidelines for demonstrating renewed commitment through actions
Resilience Section: Processes for learning from breaches and building stronger systems
Safety Section: Methods for rebuilding psychological safety and preventing future breaches

Maintaining Psychological Safety through Conflict

One of the biggest misconceptions about psychological safety is that it means avoiding conflict. Proper psychological safety enables productive conflict. It creates an environment where people feel safe to disagree, to challenge ideas, and to surface problems before they become crises.

The organizations with the strongest psychological safety aren't those with the least conflict; they're those that have learned to navigate conflict in ways that strengthen rather than damage relationships. They understand that conflict, when handled well, can deepen trust by demonstrating that relationships can survive disagreement.

This requires a fundamental shift in how we think about conflict. Instead of viewing conflict as a threat to psychological safety, we need to see it as an opportunity to strengthen it. Instead of avoiding difficult conversations, we need to develop the skills to have them well.

The key is distinguishing between productive conflict and destructive conflict. Productive conflict focuses on ideas, decisions, and outcomes. It's characterized by:

- **Respect for Persons:** Even when disagreeing strongly with someone's ideas, maintaining respect for them as a person
- **Focus on Issues:** Keeping the discussion centered on the specific issue at hand rather than expanding to broader character judgments

- **Shared Goals:** Remembering that everyone is ultimately working toward the same organizational objectives
- **Learning Orientation:** Approaching conflict as an opportunity to learn and improve rather than as a battle to be won
- **Process Discipline:** Following agreed-upon processes for decision-making and conflict resolution

Destructive conflict, on the other hand, becomes personal. It's characterized by:

- **Personal Attacks:** Shifting from critiquing ideas to attacking character
- **Generalization:** Using words like "always" and "never" to make broad character judgments
- **Win-Lose Mentality:** Viewing conflict as a zero-sum game where someone must lose
- **Emotional Escalation:** Allowing emotions to drive the conversation rather than facts and reasoning
- **Process Abandonment:** Ignoring established processes when they become inconvenient

The TIRS model helps us navigate this distinction:

Trust: We can disagree with someone's ideas while still trusting their intentions and competence

Integrity: We maintain our values and commitments even when under pressure from conflict

Resilience: We view conflict as an opportunity to strengthen relationships rather than damage them

Safety: We create conditions where people feel safe to express disagreement and surface problems

Building this capability requires developing what I call "conflict competence": the ability to engage in productive conflict while maintaining and even strengthening relationships. This competence has several key components:

Emotional Regulation: The ability to manage your own emotions during conflict so that you can respond thoughtfully rather than reactively. This doesn't mean suppressing emotions, it means being aware of them and choosing how to express them constructively.

Perspective Taking: The ability to understand and articulate the other person's point of view, even when you disagree with it. This demonstrates respect and often reveals common ground that wasn't initially apparent.

Issue Framing: The ability to frame conflicts in terms of shared goals and mutual interests rather than as personal battles. This helps keep the focus on problem-solving rather than winning.

Process Management: The ability to suggest and follow structured approaches to working through disagreements. This might include things like agreeing on ground rules, taking breaks when emotions run high, or bringing in neutral facilitators for complex issues.

Recovery Skills: The ability to repair relationships when conflicts don't go well. This includes apologizing when appropriate, acknowledging when you've made mistakes, and taking steps to rebuild trust when it's been damaged.

These skills aren't innate, they need to be developed through practice and feedback. The organizations that maintain psychological safety through conflict are those that invest in building these capabilities systematically across their leadership teams.

The Resilience Grid: Mapping Organizational Trust Vulnerabilities

To build truly resilient trust, organizations need to understand their trust vulnerabilities, the areas where trust is most likely to break down and the potential impact of those breakdowns. The Resilience Grid is a tool for mapping these vulnerabilities and developing targeted strategies to address them.

The Resilience Grid has two dimensions:

Likelihood: How likely is a trust breach in this area? This is based on factors like:

- Historical patterns of trust issues
- Current stress levels and pressures
- Complexity of relationships and dependencies
- Clarity of expectations and accountability
- Quality of communication and feedback systems

Impact: If a trust breach occurs in this area, what would be the impact? This includes:
- Number of people affected
- Criticality of affected relationships
- Potential operational disruption
- Difficulty of recovery
- Potential for cascading effects

By plotting different areas of organizational trust on this grid, leaders can identify their highest-risk areas and prioritize their trust-building and breach-prevention efforts accordingly.

High Likelihood, High Impact (Critical Zone): These are the areas that require immediate attention and ongoing monitoring. They represent the greatest threat to organizational trust and should have the most robust prevention and response systems.

High Likelihood, Low Impact (Monitor Zone): These areas need regular attention but don't require the same level of investment as critical zone items. They should be monitored for patterns that might indicate growing impact.

Low Likelihood, High Impact (Prepare Zone): These are the "black swan" events that could be devastating if they occur but are relatively unlikely. They require contingency planning but not day-to-day attention.

Low Likelihood, Low Impact (Accept Zone): These areas can generally be accepted as normal business risks without special attention, though they should still be included in regular trust assessments (Figure 4.3).

The TIRS model helps identify what to plot on the grid (Table 4.1):

Table 4.1 TIRS Diagnostics

DIAGNOSTIC LENS	KEY QUESTIONS
Trust Vulnerabilities	Where are relationships most fragile? Where is confidence in others' reliability lowest?
Integrity Risks	Where are pressures to compromise values highest? Where are expectations least clear?
Resilience Gaps	Where is recovery capability weakest? Where are the single points of failure most exposed?
Safety Threats	Where do people feel least safe to speak up? Where are the most significant barriers to open communication?

Risk Category	Description
High Likelihood, High Impact (Critical Zone) Requires immediate attention and ongoing monitoring. Represents the greatest threat to organizational trust and demands robust prevention and response systems.	**High Likelihood, Low Impact** (Monitor Zone) Needs regular attention but less investment than critical items. Monitor for patterns that may signal growing impact.
Low Likelihood, High Impact (Prepare Zone) Rare but potentially devastating events. Requires contingency planning, not daily oversight.	**Low Likelihood, Low Impact** (Accept Zone) Normal business risks that can be accepted with minimal attention, though still included in trust assessments.

Figure 4.3 Risk category map.

Once vulnerabilities are mapped, organizations can develop targeted strategies by zone (Figure 4.4):

Critical Zone Strategies:

- Implement enhanced monitoring and early warning systems
- Develop detailed breach response protocols
- Assign dedicated resources for ongoing trust maintenance
- Conduct regular trust assessments and stakeholder feedback sessions
- Create redundancy to reduce single points of failure

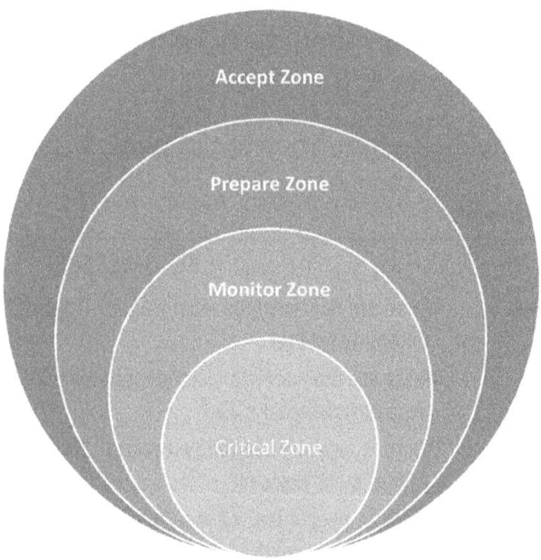

Figure 4.4 Trust zones.

Monitor Zone Strategies:

- Establish regular check-in processes
- Create feedback mechanisms to detect changes in impact potential
- Develop basic response protocols
- Include in regular risk assessments

Prepare Zone Strategies:

- Develop contingency plans for potential breaches
- Identify resources that could be quickly mobilized if needed
- Create communication templates for crises
- Establish relationships with external resources (consultants, mediators, etc.)

Accept Zone Strategies:

- Include in annual trust assessments
- Monitor for changes that might move items to other quadrants
- Maintain basic documentation and contact information

The Resilience Grid should be updated regularly as organizational conditions change. What starts as a low-risk area can quickly become high-risk if circumstances change, and vice versa.

Breach Repair Checklist and Implementation Guide

The Breach Repair Checklist is a practical tool that leaders can use when trust breakdowns occur. It's designed to be used in the immediate aftermath of a breach to ensure that critical steps aren't missed during what is often an emotionally charged and chaotic time.

Immediate Response (First 24 Hours):

- **Stop and Assess:** Before taking any action, take time to understand what happened and who was affected. Avoid the temptation to react immediately.
- **Take Responsibility:** Acknowledge your role in the breach without making excuses or shifting blame. Focus on impact, not intent.
- **Ensure Safety:** Make sure that no one is in immediate danger (physical, emotional, or professional) as a result of the breach.

- **Contain the Damage:** Take immediate steps to prevent the breach from causing additional harm or spreading to other relationships.
- **Notify Key Stakeholders:** Inform relevant people about the breach and your initial response. Don't wait until you have all the answers.
- **Document the Incident:** Create a factual record of what happened, when, and who was involved. This will be important for later analysis.

Short-Term Response (First Week):

- **Conduct Stakeholder Analysis:** Identify everyone who was affected by the breach and assess the impact on each relationship.
- **Gather Additional Information:** Interview affected parties to understand the full scope and impact of the breach.
- **Develop Initial Recovery Plan:** Create a preliminary plan for addressing the breach and rebuilding trust.
- **Communicate Regularly:** Provide updates to affected stakeholders about your analysis and recovery efforts.
- **Begin Immediate Repairs:** Start taking concrete actions to address the most urgent aspects of the breach.
- **Seek Support:** Engage coaches, mentors, or other resources to help you navigate the recovery process effectively.

Medium-Term Response (First Month):

- **Complete Root Cause Analysis:** Conduct a thorough analysis of what caused the breach and what systemic factors contributed to it.
- **Finalize Recovery Plan:** Develop a comprehensive plan with specific actions, timelines, and success metrics.
- **Implement System Changes:** Make necessary changes to processes, structures, or systems that contributed to the breach.
- **Begin Trust Rebuilding Activities:** Start the patient work of demonstrating renewed trustworthiness through consistent actions.
- **Establish Monitoring Systems:** Create ways to track your progress and get feedback on your recovery efforts.

- **Communicate Progress:** Provide regular updates to stakeholders about your recovery efforts and progress.

Long-Term Response (Ongoing):

- **Maintain Consistent Actions:** Continue demonstrating trustworthiness through daily behaviors and decisions.
- **Monitor Trust Levels:** Regularly assess whether trust is being rebuilt through surveys, feedback, and observation.
- **Adjust Recovery Efforts:** Modify your approach based on feedback and results.
- **Share Learnings:** Help others learn from your experience by sharing what you've learned about trust recovery.
- **Prevent Recurrence:** Maintain the system changes and new behaviors that prevent similar breaches.
- **Celebrate Progress:** Acknowledge milestones in the recovery process while remaining committed to ongoing improvement.

The TIRS model provides a framework for organizing these activities (Figure 4.5):

Competitive Advantage through Resilient Trust

While most leadership developments focus on building trust, the real competitive advantage comes from building resilient trust that can withstand the inevitable stresses and conflicts of organizational

Figure 4.5 Trust activities map.

life. Organizations that master this capability not only survive trust breaches but also emerge from them stronger and more cohesive than before (Table 4.2).

This resilience becomes a significant competitive advantage in several ways:

Table 4.2

DIMENSION	RESILIENT TRUST OUTCOME
Faster Recovery from Setbacks	Swift bounce-back from failures and shocks; focus shifts from blame to learning and growth.
Higher Risk Tolerance	Psychological safety fuels intelligent risk-taking, innovation, and adaptive agility.
Better Decision Making	Honest communication enhances the flow of information and facilitates more informed decisions at all levels.
Stronger Stakeholder Relationships	Stakeholders gain confidence in the organization's integrity and problem-solving capacity.
Reduced Turnover	Employees tend to stay longer where trust enables constructive conflict resolution and ensures safety.
Enhanced Reputation	A reputation for handling breaches effectively attracts top talent, partners, and new opportunities.

Building resilient trust isn't easy, and it doesn't happen quickly. It requires sustained effort, systematic thinking, and the courage to face brutal truths about organizational weaknesses. But for organizations willing to make this investment, the payoff is substantial: a level of organizational trust that becomes a truly competitive advantage in an increasingly complex and uncertain business environment.

Conclusion: The Antifragile Organization

As we conclude this exploration of trust resilience, it's essential to understand that we're not just talking about bouncing back from trust breaches; we're talking about building organizations that grow stronger through adversity. This is what Nassim Taleb calls "antifragility": the property of systems that improve when exposed to stress.

Most organizations are fragile when it comes to trust. A single major breach can shatter relationships and destroy years of careful relationship building. Some organizations and teams are resilient. They demonstrate the ability to recover from trust breaches and return to their previous state. But the truly exceptional organizations and teams are antifragile; they use trust breaches as opportunities to build even stronger, more resilient relationships than they had before.

This antifragility doesn't happen by accident. It requires intentional design, systematic preparation, and the courage to face the uncomfortable truth that trust will break. But for organizations willing to do this work, the reward is extraordinary: a level of organizational trust that becomes stronger, not weaker, when tested by adversity (Table 4.3).

The TIRS model provides the foundation for building this antifragile trust:

Table 4.3

CORE PRINCIPLE	DEFINING INSIGHT
Trust	Deepens through testing rather than breaking under pressure
Integrity	Becomes more evident in difficult times than in easy ones
Resilience	Transforms setbacks into opportunities for growth
Safety	Enables people to take the risks necessary for innovation and excellence

In our next chapter, we'll explore how to scale these principles across entire organizations, building cultures where anti-fragile trust becomes not just an individual capability but an organizational competency. We'll examine how to create systems and structures that support resilient trust at scale, and how to measure and maintain these capabilities over time.

The journey toward antifragile trust is not easy, but it's essential for any organization that wants to thrive in an increasingly complex and uncertain world. The organizations that master this capability won't just survive the inevitable trust breaches; they'll use them as stepping stones to even higher levels of performance and relationship quality.

5

The Human Firewall

Culture Is Security

Most leaders treat culture like wallpaper, decorative, ambient, something you notice only when it's peeling. They talk about "culture fit" in hiring meetings and plaster values on conference-room walls, then wonder why their organizations hemorrhage trust when the pressure mounts. Here's what they miss: **culture isn't background noise. Culture is your first line of defense.**

In cybersecurity, a firewall is the barrier between trusted internal networks and untrusted external threats. It monitors traffic, blocks malicious actors, and creates a protective perimeter around valuable assets. Your organizational culture functions precisely the same way. When culture is strong, and trust is woven into daily behavior, your people become active defenders of organizational integrity. When culture is weak, every interaction becomes a potential breach point.

The difference is this: digital firewalls are binary. They follow rules. They can't detect nuances, read a room, or sense when something feels off. Humans can. Your people are sophisticated detection systems capable of identifying threats that no algorithm could catch: the slight shift in a colleague's tone that signals burnout, the pattern of small corner-cutting that precedes major failure, the subtle exclusion that indicates deeper dysfunction.

But here's the catch: this only works if you treat your people like the critical security infrastructure they are. You can't install a firewall and forget about it. You can't hire good people, assume they'll "get" the culture, and expect them to protect organizational trust without systems, training, and support. Culture-as-security requires intentional design, constant monitoring, and regular updates.

This chapter is about building that human firewall. It's about transforming culture from vague and aspirational to operational and defensive. Because when trust fails in organizations, it's rarely a single

DOI: 10.1201/9781003688815-6

catastrophic breach. It's a thousand small compromises that nobody noticed, nobody named, and nobody stopped.

What It Means to Be a Human Firewall

Think about what a firewall does. It doesn't just block obvious attacks. It monitors patterns. It detects anomalies. It distinguishes between legitimate traffic and suspicious activity. It creates logs. It escalates threats. It operates continuously, not just when someone remembers to check it.

Now imagine your team members functioning the same way.

Being a human firewall means you're an active sensor, not a passive participant. You're not just doing your job; you're monitoring the integrity of the environment while you work. You notice when someone who usually speaks up goes quiet. You flag when a process that should require three approvals suddenly requires only one. You detect when the language in meetings shifts from "we" to "they." You sense when the pressure to hit numbers starts to override the commitment to quality.

This isn't about creating a surveillance culture or encouraging people to police each other. It's about cultivating collective responsibility for the system's health. In high-trust organizations, everyone understands that protecting trust is part of their role, regardless of their title.

Consider what happened at a mid-sized financial services firm we'll call Meridian Capital. During a routine project debrief, a junior analyst named James noticed something odd. The numbers in the client presentation didn't match the numbers in the internal analysis. Not by much, just enough that someone who wasn't paying close attention might miss it. The senior partner leading the project brushed it off: "We rounded for clarity. The client doesn't need that level of detail."

James had a choice. He could accept the explanation and move on. Most people would. But James had been through Meridian's culture training, which explicitly framed every employee as a "trust defender." The training didn't just tell people to speak up; it gave them the language, process, and protection to do so. James used the firm's "integrity escalation" protocol to flag the discrepancy to the compliance team.

The investigation revealed that the senior partner had been systematically adjusting figures across multiple client accounts—not enough to trigger automated alerts, but enough to mask underperformance and protect his bonus. James's willingness to act as a human firewall prevented what could have become a massive breach of trust with clients and regulators.

Here's what made this possible: Meridian had designed its culture so that being a human firewall wasn't heroic; it was normal. James wasn't a whistleblower risking his career. He was an employee using a standard protocol that the organization had built, tested, and reinforced.

Every team member is an active sensor, meaning creating conditions for people to detect, interpret, and respond to trust threats. This requires three things:

First, **awareness.** People need to understand what trust threats look like in their specific context. Not abstract principles, but concrete patterns: What does corner-cutting look like in your industry? What does exclusion sound like in your meetings? What does pressure-driven compromise feel like in your workflow?

Second, **agency.** People need clear pathways to act on what they detect. If you see something wrong but don't know what to do about it, you'll rationalize it away. Human firewalls need protocols, not just principles.

Third, **protection.** People need to know that acting as a trust defender won't make them a target. This means visible, consistent protection from retaliation and clear consequences for those who retaliate.

The power of human firewalls is that they detect threats that systems can't. Automated monitoring can detect fraudulent transactions. It can't catch the meeting where someone's idea gets credited to someone else. It can't detect a pattern in which a manager consistently gives stretch assignments to some team members but not others. It can't sense the shift in team dynamics when psychological safety erodes.

Humans detect tone. They notice when someone's communication style changes, when the colleague who usually writes detailed emails starts sending terse one-liners, when the manager who used to ask questions starts issuing directives, when the team that used to debate ideas starts nodding in silent agreement.

Humans detect pattern changes. They recognize when the informal rules shift, when "we always loop in legal" becomes "let's move fast and ask forgiveness later," when "we debate decisions" becomes "the boss has already decided," when "we celebrate learning from failure" becomes "we don't talk about what went wrong."

Humans detect subtle violations. They feel the difference between a meeting that runs long because of genuine engagement and one that runs long because someone is dominating the conversation. They sense when someone's being excluded from information they need. They notice when credit flows up, but accountability flows down.

This is why culture is secure. Your people are your most sophisticated detection system. If you train them, empower them, and protect them.

Micro-Behavior Monitoring and Cultural Drift

Culture doesn't collapse overnight. It drifts.

Drift is the slow, almost imperceptible movement away from stated values and toward expedient behaviors. It's what happens when small compromises compound into new norms. It's the organizational equivalent of scope creep or technical debt, invisible until it's catastrophic.

In cybersecurity, drift is a known threat. Systems drift from their secure baseline configurations. Patches don't get applied. Permissions accumulate. Security protocols get bypassed "just this once" until the bypass becomes standard practice. Innovative security teams monitor drift constantly because they know that major breaches rarely start with sophisticated attacks. They begin with drift.

Organizational trust works the same way. Major trust failures: fraud, harassment, discrimination, and ethical collapse rarely come out of nowhere. They're preceded by months or years of micro-behavior that signal drift: small violations that go unaddressed, minor corner-cutting that gets normalized, subtle exclusions that become patterns.

Micro-behaviors are the atomic units of culture. They're the small, everyday actions that signal what's really valued: who speaks first in meetings, whose ideas get explored versus dismissed, how people respond when someone admits a mistake, whether deadlines trump quality, how information flows, who gets access to leaders, what gets celebrated, and what gets ignored.

Here's the dangerous thing about micro-behaviors: individually, they seem insignificant. Collectively, they define reality.

Consider these examples of **negative micro-behaviors** that signal drift:

- A leader checks their phone while a team member presents, signaling that some people's contributions matter less than others.
- Someone takes credit for a collaborative effort using "I" instead of "we," and nobody corrects the record.
- A meeting starts without waiting for remote participants to connect, establishing that in-person presence is what counts.
- Someone interrupts a colleague, and the interruption is allowed to stand rather than redirected.
- A question about ethics or risk is met with "let's take that offline," signaling that concerns aren't welcome in public forums.
- Feedback is delivered as criticism without context or coaching, teaching people that mistakes are punished rather than learned from.
- A deadline is moved up without consultation, demonstrating that urgency trumps input.
- Someone makes a joke at another person's expense, and the room laughs instead of redirecting.

None of these behaviors, in isolation, destroys trust. But when they repeat, go unaddressed, and become "just how things are," they create drift. The organization says it values collaboration, but the micro-behavior rewards individual heroics. It says it values diverse perspectives, but the micro-behaviors privilege certain voices. It says it values integrity, but the micro-behaviors reward speed over thoroughness.

Now consider **positive micro-behaviors** that reinforce trust:

- A leader pauses a meeting to invite input from someone who hasn't spoken yet explicitly.
- Someone corrects attribution in real-time: "That was actually Sarah's idea. Sarah, can you walk us through your thinking?"
- A manager responds to a mistake by asking "What did we learn?" before asking "What went wrong?"
- Someone names a concern in a meeting, and the leader thanks them for raising it before addressing the substance.
- A decision is explained with clear reasoning, even when the decision is unpopular.

- Someone admits uncertainty: "I don't know, let me find out, and it's treated as professionalism, not weakness.
- A team celebrates a project by specifically acknowledging contributions from support roles, not just visible leaders.
- Someone asks, "Who else should be in this conversation?" before making a decision that affects others.

These micro-behaviors seem small. But they're the code that writes your culture. They're the daily proof of what your organization actually values, regardless of what your values statement says.

The danger of drift is that it's invisible until it's not. You overlook the culture shift because each shift is tiny. The meeting that starts five minutes late becomes ten minutes late, then becomes "we'll start when everyone gets here," and then becomes "time doesn't really matter." The decision to skip one approval becomes a pattern of skipping approvals, which becomes "we don't really need that process." The feedback that's a little harsh becomes consistently harsh feedback, becomes "that's just how things are here."

By the time drift becomes visible, it's deeply embedded. Correcting it requires not just changing behavior but overcoming the organizational inertia that's built up around the new normal.

Creating systems that prompt people to notice and flag microviolations requires making the invisible visible. This means:

Building a shared language for micro-behaviors. You can't address what you can't name. High-trust organizations develop specific vocabulary for the behaviors that matter. At one tech company, they use the terms "steamrolling" to describe when someone dominates a conversation and "parking lot dumping" to describe when concerns are deferred without follow-up. Having names for these patterns makes them discussable.

Establishing observation protocols. Some teams designate a rotating "culture observer" role for meetings; someone whose job is to watch for micro-behaviors and provide feedback afterward. This isn't about policing; it's about creating structured attention to patterns that are usually overlooked.

Creating regular reflection rituals. One consulting firm ends every project with a "micro-behavior retrospective," in which the team identifies three positive micro-behaviors to amplify and three negative ones to address. This builds the muscle of noticing and naming.

Modeling the naming of drift. Leaders who notice and name drift in real-time, "I'm noticing we've started these meetings late three times in a row; what's happening?", permit others to do the same. The leader who says, "I just interrupted you, I'm sorry, please continue," teaches the team that interruptions are violations worth addressing.

Tracking patterns, not just incidents. One incident of someone being interrupted might be random. Five incidents in three meetings are a pattern. Systems that track micro-behaviors over time can reveal drift that's invisible in the moment.

The goal isn't perfect. The goal is **awareness and correction.** Drift is inevitable in any human system. What matters is whether you have the cultural infrastructure to detect it and the organizational will to address it.

Inclusion as an Early Warning System

Here's a truth that makes many leaders uncomfortable: **inclusion isn't just a moral imperative or a business advantage. It's a security feature.**

In cybersecurity, redundancy and diversity are fundamental principles. You don't rely on a single point of failure. You don't use identical systems across your entire infrastructure because a vulnerability in one becomes a vulnerability in all of them. You build in multiple detection mechanisms because different threats require different sensors.

Inclusion works the same way. When your organization includes diverse perspectives, experiences, and identities, you're building a more sophisticated detection system. Different people notice different things. They interpret signals differently. They're sensitive to other patterns. This isn't about political correctness; it's about operational effectiveness.

Excluded voices are the canary in the coal mine. They detect trust threats earlier because they're more attuned to the subtle signals that something's wrong. When you're part of the dominant group, you can afford to miss signals. When you're not, you can't. You learn to read rooms, detect shifts in tone, notice who's included and who's not, and sense when the rules are changing.

This means that when people from marginalized groups feel unsafe speaking up, your organization loses its most sensitive early warning system. You're flying blind to threats that could be detected if you were listening.

Consider what happened at a healthcare technology company called Company X. The company had developed an AI-powered diagnostic tool that was being piloted in several hospital systems. The tool was performing well in testing, and the leadership team was preparing for a significant product launch.

During a pre-launch review, Aisha, one of the few Black engineers on the team, raised a concern. She'd noticed that the training data was predominantly from patients at well-resourced urban hospitals. She worried that the tool might not perform as well for patients in under-resourced settings or for patients with different demographic characteristics. She suggested delaying the launch to expand the training data.

The response from leadership was dismissive. "We've tested this extensively. The accuracy rates are excellent. We can refine it after launch." Aisha pushed back, but she was outvoted. The tool launched.

Six months later, investigative journalists revealed that Company X's diagnostic tool was significantly less accurate for Black patients and patients in rural settings. The company faced lawsuits, regulatory scrutiny, and massive reputational damage. The CEO was forced to resign.

Here's the critical point: Aisha detected the threat early. She had the expertise and the perspective to see what others missed. But the organization's culture didn't treat her concern as valuable intelligence; it treated it as an obstacle to overcome. The lack of inclusion wasn't just a diverse problem. It was a security failure.

When people feel unsafe speaking up, trust vulnerabilities go undetected. This happens in several ways:

Perspective blindness. Homogeneous groups develop shared blind spots. They all miss the same things because they're all looking from the same angle. Diverse groups are more likely to spot threats because someone in the group has a vantage point that others don't.

Silence is a risk. When people don't feel safe raising concerns, it's because they've been dismissed before, worried about being labeled "difficult," or don't see people like them in leadership, they stop speaking up. The concerns don't go away; they go underground. The organization loses access to critical information.

Conformity pressure. In low-inclusion environments, people learn to conform to dominant norms to survive. This means they stop bringing their complete perspective to work. They self-censor. They go along to get along. The organization thinks it has consensus when it actually has compliance.

Delayed detection. Trust threats that could be caught early go undetected; they only become visible after they've metastasized into significant problems. By the time the danger is visible to everyone, it's much more complex and more expensive to address.

Creating concrete mechanisms for ensuring inclusion functions as detection requires intentional design:

Structured solicitation of dissent. Don't just invite people to speak; actively solicit disagreement. One executive team uses a "designated dissenter" role in major decisions, rotating responsibility so that someone is explicitly tasked with articulating the strongest case against the proposed course of action. This normalizes dissent and ensures that contrary perspectives are heard.

Diverse decision-making bodies. Ensure that decision-makers represent diverse perspectives and experiences. This isn't tokenism; it's building a more sophisticated detection system. When the people in the room have different backgrounds, they're more likely to identify various risks.

Anonymous feedback channels with visible follow-up. Create ways for people to raise concerns without fear of being identified, while demonstrating that these concerns are taken seriously. If anonymous feedback disappears into a black hole, people stop providing it. If they see concerns investigated and addressed, they trust the system.

Inclusion metrics tied to risk management. Track inclusion is not just an HR metric but also a risk indicator. Measure: Do people from different backgrounds speak up at equal rates in meetings? Are concerns raised by people from marginalized groups addressed as seriously as concerns raised by others? Are diverse perspectives represented in key decisions?

Psychological safety as infrastructure. Build specific practices that create safety: leaders admitting mistakes, concerns being thanked before being addressed, disagreement being rewarded, and questions being treated as valuable rather than threatening. These aren't soft skills; they're security protocols.

One financial services firm implemented what they call "perspective audits" for major decisions. Before finalizing any significant strategic choice, they convene a diverse group specifically tasked with identifying risks and blind spots. The group includes people from different levels, functions, backgrounds, and tenures. Their job isn't to approve the decision; it's to stress-test it from multiple angles. This practice caught numerous potential problems before they became actual crises.

The point is this: **inclusion is not separate from trust. Inclusion is how you build a trust detection system sophisticated enough to catch threats before they become breaches.** When you exclude voices, you're not just creating a culture problem; you're making a security vulnerability.

Team-Based Trust Rituals

Individual responsibility for trust is necessary but insufficient. You can't build a human firewall by telling each person to be trustworthy and hoping it works out. You need **collective practices that reinforce trust as a team capability, not just an individual virtue.** This is where rituals come in.

Rituals are repeated practices that encode values into behavior. They're the organizational equivalent of muscle memory, becoming automatic through repetition. In high-trust organizations, rituals serve several functions: they make trust tangible, create shared experience, establish rhythm and predictability, and reinforce what matters.

The key is that rituals must be **specific, regular, and meaningful**. Vague commitments to "communicate better" don't change behavior. Specific practices, repeated consistently, do (Figure 5.1).

Here are team-based trust rituals that work across different organizational contexts.

Figure 5.1 Team-based trust rituals.

The Trust Check-In

At the start of each team meeting, spend three minutes on a structured check-in where each person shares: one thing that's building their trust in the team right now, and one thing that's testing it. This isn't therapy; **it's operational intelligence**. It surfaces issues early, celebrates what's working, and normalizes explicit discussion of trust.

A marketing team at a consumer goods company uses this ritual religiously. In one check-in, a team member named Marcus shared that his trust was being tested because he'd submitted a campaign proposal two weeks earlier and hadn't heard any feedback. The creative director realized the proposal had gotten lost in her inbox. She apologized, reviewed it during the meeting, and they established a new protocol: all proposals get acknowledged within 48 hours, even if full feedback takes longer. A minor issue that could have festered into resentment got caught and addressed immediately.

The Attribution Practice

In any meeting where work is discussed, the team explicitly practices accurate attribution. When someone references an idea, they name its originator. When talking about success, they identify all contributors, not just the most visible. When presenting to external stakeholders, they use "we" language and specifically call out individual contributions.

This ritual does two things: it ensures that credit flows accurately, which builds trust, and it trains people to notice and value contributions that might otherwise be invisible. One software development team found that this practice revealed how much of their success depended on their QA engineer, whose work had been consistently undervalued. Making her contributions visible changed team dynamics and retention.

The Mistake Harvest

Once a month, the team gathers to "harvest" mistakes, to explicitly share what went wrong, what was learned, and what's changing as a result. The ritual has a specific structure: each person shares one mistake, the team asks curious questions (not judgmental ones), and the group identifies systemic factors that contributed to the error.

This ritual normalizes failure as part of learning and shifts focus from individual blame to system improvement. A product team at a SaaS company credits this practice with catching a significant security vulnerability. During a mistake harvest, a developer shared that he'd almost pushed code to production without proper review because he was rushing to meet a deadline. The team realized that their sprint planning consistently created time pressure, encouraging corner-cutting. They restructured their process, building in buffer time for proper review.

Perspective Rotation

For major decisions or projects, team members rotate through different perspective-taking roles. One person plays "customer advocate," another plays "risk manager," another plays "resource guardian," and another plays "innovation champion." Each person argues from their assigned perspective, ensuring that multiple angles are considered.

This ritual prevents groupthink and ensures that diverse viewpoints are heard even in homogeneous teams. A hospital leadership team used this practice when deciding whether to implement a new patient management system. The person playing "frontline staff advocate" raised concerns about training time and workflow disruption that the leadership team had underestimated. They adjusted the implementation timeline and training plan, avoiding what could have been a disastrous rollout.

The Feedback Loop Close

Many teams are good at gathering feedback but terrible at closing the loop, letting people know what happened with their input. This ritual requires that, whenever feedback is solicited, there be a scheduled follow-up in which the team shares: what feedback was received, what decisions were made, how the input influenced those decisions, and what feedback couldn't be incorporated and why.

These rituals build trust by demonstrating that input matters and that the process is transparent. A nonprofit organization implemented this practice after employee surveys revealed low trust in leadership. Within six months, survey scores improved significantly, not because leadership made every change employees wanted, but because employees could see that their feedback was genuinely considered and that decisions were explained.

The Trust Retrospective

At the end of major projects or quarters, teams conduct a retrospective focused specifically on trust: What built trust during this period? What damaged it? What do we want to continue? What do we want to change? The conversation is structured, documented, and translated into specific commitments.

An engineering team at a manufacturing company does this quarterly. In one retrospective, they identified that trust had been damaged when a manager made a significant technical decision without consulting the team. The manager acknowledged the mistake and established a new protocol: decisions with an impact threshold above a certain level require team input. The retrospective turned a trust breach into a trust-building moment by addressing it explicitly and systematically.

The key to effective rituals is that they must be:

Consistent. Rituals work through repetition. Doing a trust check-in once doesn't change culture. Doing it at the start of every meeting for six months does.

Structured. Vague invitations to "share concerns" often result in silence. Specific prompts and formats make participation easier and more equitable.

Protected. Rituals must be protected from the pressure to skip them when things get busy. The moment you forget the trust check-in because you're "too busy," you signal that trust is optional.

Adapted. Rituals should evolve based on what the team learns. If practice isn't working, modify it. The goal is effectiveness, not rigidity.

Modeled. Leaders must participate fully in trust rituals, not just facilitate them. When a leader shares a mistake during the mistake harvest or acknowledges a trust concern during the check-in, it permits others to do the same.

Trust rituals transform trust from an abstract value into a concrete practice. They create the conditions where being a human firewall isn't an individual burden, it's a collective capability.

Tools: Inclusion Scorecard and Culture Temperature Check

Theory without tools is inspiration without implementation. Here are two practical frameworks you can use immediately to strengthen your human firewall.

Inclusion Scorecard

The Inclusion Scorecard helps you assess whether inclusion is functioning as an early warning system in your organization. It measures inclusion not as a demographic metric but as an operational capability (Table 5.1).

Table 5.1 Dimensions to Measure

CATEGORY	SCORE RANGE (0–5)	CRITERIA DESCRIPTION
1. Voice Distribution	**0**	Meetings are dominated by the same few voices; others rarely speak.
	3	Most people speak, but some voices are consistently more influential.
	5	Speaking time and influence are distributed equitably; all voices are actively solicited and valued.
2. Idea Attribution	**0**	Ideas are regularly misattributed; credit flows to senior or dominant group members regardless of origin.
	3	Attribution is generally accurate but requires conscious effort; some contributions go unrecognized.
	5	Attribution is automatic and accurate; all contributions are explicitly acknowledged.
3. Dissent Safety	**0**	Disagreement is punished or discouraged; people self-censor to avoid negative consequences.
	3	Dissent is theoretically welcome but practically risky; people are cautious about speaking up.
	5	Dissent is actively solicited and rewarded; disagreement is treated as valuable input.
4. Decision Representation	**0**	Homogeneous groups make key decisions; affected stakeholders are not consulted.
	3	Diverse perspectives are sometimes included but not systematically.

(Continued)

Table 5.1 Dimensions to Measure *(Continued)*

CATEGORY	SCORE RANGE (0–5)	CRITERIA DESCRIPTION
	5	Decision-making bodies consistently include diverse perspectives; those affected by decisions have meaningful input.
5. Feedback Responsiveness	**0**	Concerns raised by marginalized group members are dismissed or ignored.
	3	Concerns are acknowledged but not always addressed; follow-through is inconsistent.
	5	Concerns are investigated seriously regardless of who raises them; patterns of dismissal are tracked and corrected.
6. Psychological Safety Indicators	**0**	People report feeling unsafe, raising concerns; fear of retaliation is common.
	3	Safety is inconsistent; it depends heavily on the specific manager or team.
	5	People consistently report feeling safe to take interpersonal risks; vulnerability is normalized.

How to Score

Assess each dimension quarterly using multiple data sources: surveys, meeting observations, focus groups, and behavioral metrics (e.g., who speaks in meetings, whose ideas get implemented, who raises concerns).

Calculate your total score (0–30) and your score by dimension.

Interpreting Results

- **25–30:** Inclusion is functioning as a strong early-warning system; maintain and refine practices
- **18–24:** Inclusion is partially effective; focus on dimensions scoring below 4
- **10–17:** Significant inclusion gaps are creating trust vulnerabilities; immediate intervention needed
- **0–9:** Inclusion is not functioning as a detection system; major cultural overhaul required

Actions to Take

For any dimension scoring below 3, implement specific interventions:

- **Voice Distribution:** Use structured turn-taking in meetings; implement "no interruption" norms; track speaking time.

- **Idea Attribution:** Practice explicit attribution; correct misattribution in real-time; celebrate accurate crediting.
- **Dissent Safety:** Create anonymous feedback channels; reward dissent publicly; track and address retaliation.
- **Decision Representation:** Audit decision-making bodies for diversity; establish consultation protocols; use perspective rotation.
- **Feedback Responsiveness:** Implement feedback loop close ritual; track response times by demographic group; address patterns of dismissal.
- **Psychological Safety:** Conduct team building focused on vulnerability; model mistake-sharing; establish clear anti-retaliation policies.

Culture Temperature Check

The Culture Temperature Check is a rapid assessment tool for detecting cultural drift before it becomes a cultural crisis. It's designed to be administered frequently (monthly or quarterly) to track trends over time.

Questions to Ask

Use a 1–5 scale (1 = strongly disagree, 5 = strongly agree) for each question:

Trust in Leadership:

1. Leaders in this organization do what they say they'll do.
2. When leaders make mistakes, they acknowledge them openly.
3. I trust that leaders have the organization's best interests at heart.
4. Leaders are transparent about the reasoning behind major decisions.

Trust in Peers:

5. I can rely on my colleagues to follow through on commitments.
6. People on my team give credit where it's due.
7. I feel comfortable asking colleagues for help when I need it.
8. Conflicts on my team are addressed constructively.

Trust in Systems:

9. Our processes and policies are applied consistently and fairly.
10. When I raise a concern, I trust it will be taken seriously.
11. Our organization's stated values align with how decisions are made.
12. I have the resources and support I need to do my job well.

Psychological Safety:

13. I feel safe speaking up with ideas, questions, or concerns.
14. It's okay to take risks and make mistakes in this organization.
15. People in this organization value diverse perspectives.
16. I can be at work without fear of negative consequences.

Micro-Behavior Indicators:

17. People in meetings listen to understand, not just to respond.
18. When someone makes a mistake, the focus is on learning, not blaming.
19. Information flows freely; I have access to what I need to know.
20. Recognition and opportunities are distributed fairly.

Frequency

Administer monthly for teams in transition or facing challenges, quarterly for stable teams. The goal is to detect trends, not just snapshots.

How to Interpret Results

Individual Scores:

- 4.0–5.0: Strong trust indicator
- 3.0–3.9: Moderate trust; monitor for decline
- 2.0–2.9: Weak trust; intervention needed
- 1.0–1.9: Trust crisis; immediate action required

Trend Analysis

More important than absolute scores are trends. A score that drops from 4.2 to 3.8 over two quarters signals drift, even if the absolute score seems acceptable.

Variance Analysis

High variance in scores (some people rating 5, others rating 1 on the same question) indicates inconsistent experience, some people feel trust, others don't. This often reveals manager-specific issues or demographic disparities.

Demographic Cuts

Analyze scores by demographic groups, tenure, level, and function. Significant disparities indicate that trust is not experienced equally, a major vulnerability.

What to Do with Results

- **Share Transparently:** Report results for the entire organization, including areas of strength and concern. Transparency about the data builds trust in the process.
- **Identify Patterns:** Look for questions with consistently low scores or declining trends. These are your priority areas.
- **Dig Deeper:** Use focus groups or interviews to understand the "why" behind the numbers. Quantitative data tells you where to look; qualitative data tells you what to do.
- **Take Visible Action:** Identify 2–3 specific changes you'll make based on the data. Communicate these changes clearly and implement them quickly. Then close the loop, tell people what changed and why.
- **Track Over Time:** Culture change is slow. Track your temperature check scores over multiple quarters to see if interventions are working.

Example in Action

A professional services firm administered the Culture Temperature Check and found that scores for "I feel safe speaking up with ideas, questions, or concerns" had dropped from 4.1 to 3.3 over two quarters. They dug deeper through focus groups and discovered that a recent restructuring had created uncertainty about roles and decision rights. People didn't know who to raise concerns to or whether their input would matter.

The firm responded by:

1. Clarifying decision-making authority in the new structure.
2. Establishing regular "office hours" where anyone could raise concerns directly about leadership.
3. Implementing the feedback loop closure ritual to demonstrate that input was valued. Within two quarters, the score had recovered to 4.0.

The Culture Temperature Check caught drift early enough to address it before it became a crisis.

The human firewall is not a metaphor. It's an operational reality. Your people are either actively defending organizational trust or passively allowing it to erode. The difference is whether you've built the culture, practices, and systems that enable them to function as trust defenders.

Culture is security. Treat it that way.

When you invest in culture with the same rigor you invest in cybersecurity, with monitoring systems, clear protocols, regular audits, and rapid response to threats, you build an organization where trust is not just valued but protected, where micro-behaviors are noticed and addressed, where inclusion functions as an early-warning system. Where rituals reinforce trust as a collective capability.

This is not soft work. This is the most challenging, most critical work of leadership. Because when your human firewall is strong, trust threats get detected and addressed before they become breaches. When it's weak, you're vulnerable to failures you won't see coming until it's too late.

The question is not whether you have a human firewall. You do. The question is whether it's functioning.

6

Trust as Code

Embedding It Everywhere

Trust needs to be hardcoded into your systems. From onboarding to procurement, this chapter teaches how to write trust into infrastructure.

When Sarah joined a rapidly scaling fintech startup as its new Chief Operating Officer, she inherited what appeared to be a success story. Revenue was up 300% year-over-year. The product was gaining traction. Investors were circling for the Series B. But within her first week, she discovered something troubling: the company had no formal process for handling customer data requests, no clear escalation path when employees witnessed potential compliance violations, and procurement decisions worth hundreds of thousands of dollars were being made in Slack DMs based on whoever had the founder's ear that day.

The company wasn't malicious. They were moving fast, and trust had become an assumption rather than an architecture.

Three months later, a junior engineer discovered that a vendor they'd hastily onboarded was storing customer data on unsecured servers in a jurisdiction with weak privacy laws. The engineer mentioned it to their manager, who said they'd "look into it." Nothing happened. Two weeks later, the engineer posted about it in the company's #random Slack channel out of frustration. By the time leadership responded, screenshots had leaked to Twitter, and the company was facing both a regulatory investigation and a customer exodus.

The cost? $4.2 million in immediate losses, 18 months of remediation work, and immeasurable damage to their reputation. The root cause wasn't a bad actor or a malicious decision. It was the absence of trust infrastructure, the systems, protocols, and mechanisms that made trustworthy behavior the default path, not the heroic exception.

DOI: 10.1201/9781003688815-7

This is what we mean when we talk about trust as code. In the previous chapters, we've explored trust as a strategic asset, examined the neuroscience of how trust forms, investigated the role of leadership in modeling trustworthy behavior, analyzed how to build trust across teams, and studied how to repair trust when it breaks. Now we're getting tactical. We're going to examine how to hardcode trust into your organization's operational DNA; in your systems, policies, procedures, and daily workflows.

Because here's the truth that most leadership books won't tell you: culture eats strategy for breakfast, but systems eat culture for lunch. You can have the most inspiring mission statement and the most charismatic leaders, but still fail. If your systems make untrustworthy behavior easy and trustworthy behavior hard, you will get untrustworthy outcomes every single time.

What Does Operational Trust Look Like?

Before we can embed trust into our systems, we need to understand what operational trust looks like in practice. It's not an abstract concept or a feeling. It's a set of observable, measurable behaviors and outcomes that emerge when your organizational infrastructure is designed to support trustworthy action.

The Trust-Action Gap

Most organizations have what I call a "trust-action gap": the distance between what they say they value and what their systems reward or enable.

You see this everywhere:

A company claims to value transparency but has a performance review system where managers are explicitly told not to share specific feedback with their direct reports "to avoid demotivating them." A healthcare organization says patient safety is its top priority, but its incident reporting system is so cumbersome that nurses routinely skip it for minor issues, leaving patterns undetected. A tech company preaches innovation but has a procurement process so Byzantine that engineers have learned to expense personal credit cards rather than wait three months for approval on a $500 tool.

Each of these gaps erodes trust. Not because anyone is lying, but because the system teaches people that the stated values aren't absolute. The system is the truth.

Operational trust, by contrast, exists when your systems close these gaps. When the most straightforward path forward is also the most trustworthy, when doing the right thing doesn't require heroism, follow the process.

The Three Markers of Trust-Embedded Systems

In my work with organizations across industries, I've identified three consistent markers that indicate trust has been successfully embedded into operational infrastructure:

1. **Transparency is the default, not the exception.**
   In trust-embedded systems, information flows freely unless there's a specific, documented reason for restriction. Meeting notes are automatically shared. Decision-making criteria are explicit. When someone asks, "Why did we decide that?" the answer is readily available, not locked in someone's head or buried in a private email thread.
   Consider how Amazon approaches this with their "narrative" culture. Before any significant decision, the team writes a six-page memo that lays out the context, the options considered, the decision criteria, and the recommendation. This isn't just about better decision-making (though it achieves that). It's about creating a system where the reasoning is transparent and auditable. Anyone can look back and understand not just what was decided, but why.
2. **Accountability is structural, not personal.**
   In organizations without a trust infrastructure, accountability is about assigning blame when things go wrong. In trust-embedded systems, accountability is built into the workflow. It's clear who owns what, what the standards are, and how performance is measured. When something fails, the system helps you understand what broke and how to fix it, not just who to fire.
   The aviation industry exemplifies this. When an incident occurs, the investigation focuses on understanding the chain of events and the system failures that enabled it. Pilots are encouraged to report their own errors through programs like NASA's Aviation Safety Reporting System, which provides

immunity from punishment in exchange for detailed incident reports. The result? An industry that has become extraordinarily safe because the system is designed to learn from mistakes, not hide them.

3. **Ethical action is easy; unethical action is hard.**

   This is perhaps the most important marker. In trust-embedded systems, friction is placed on the wrong behavior, not the correct behavior. It's easy to escalate a concern. It's easy to flag a potential problem. It's easy to say, "I need more time to do this right." What's hard is cutting corners, hiding information, or making decisions without proper review.

   Think about how modern code repositories work. If you want to merge code into the main branch, you typically need peer review, passing automated tests, and, sometimes, security scans. The system makes it easy to do the right thing (submit for review, wait for tests) and hard to do the risky thing (push directly to production). This isn't about not trusting developers. It's about creating infrastructure that supports good outcomes.

The Operational Trust Audit

Before you can embed trust more deeply, you need to understand where you currently stand. Here's a quick diagnostic you can run on any process or system in your organization:

The Five Questions:

1. **Visibility:** Can people see how decisions are made in this area? If I'm new to the organization, can I understand the logic behind it?
2. **Voice:** Do people have a clear, low-friction way to raise concerns or suggest improvements? What happens when they do?
3. **Consistency:** Does this system produce similar outcomes for similar inputs, or does it depend heavily on who you know or who's in the room?
4. **Learning:** When something goes wrong, does the system help us understand why and improve, or does it focus on blame and punishment?
5. **Alignment:** Does following this process make it easier or harder to live up to our stated values?

Run your onboarding process through these questions. Or your expense approval system. Or your promotion criteria. You'll quickly identify where trust is embedded and where it's absent.

I worked with a professional services firm that used this exercise as part of their client engagement process. They discovered that their system for flagging potential conflicts of interest was so cumbersome. It required three separate forms and approvals from people who were often traveling. Partners had started making judgment calls on their own rather than going through the process. The system was creating exactly the risk it was designed to prevent. Once they saw this clearly, they redesigned the process to be a simple, two-minute online form with automatic routing and a 24-hour turnaround commitment. Compliance went from 60% to 97% in six months.

Writing Trust into Systems, Policies, and Procedures

Now let's get specific about how to embed trust into your organizational infrastructure. This isn't about creating more bureaucracy or slowing things down. It's about designing systems that make trustworthy behavior the path of least resistance.

The Onboarding Trust Foundation

Onboarding is where you set the template for how trust works in your organization. It's not just about teaching people what to do; it's about teaching them how decisions get made, how concerns get raised, and what the organization values versus what it says it values.

Most onboarding programs fail at this. They're a fire hose of information about benefits, tools, and org charts, but they don't teach the invisible curriculum.

Here's how to redesign onboarding as a trust-building system:

Make the implicit explicit. Create a "How We Work" guide that documents not just your processes but your principles. How do we make decisions? What do we do when we disagree? How do we handle mistakes? What does "transparency" mean here? What's shared and what's not, and why?

One software company I advised created a "Decision-Making Matrix" that they share on day one. It clearly maps out which decisions can be made autonomously at each level, which require consultation, and which require approval. New employees aren't left guessing whether they need permission or forgiveness. The system tells them.

Build in early trust tests. Design your onboarding to include small, low-stakes opportunities for new employees to practice the behaviors you want to see. Ask them to give feedback on the onboarding process itself. Have them shadow a decision-making meeting and then debrief on their observations. Please give them a small project that requires collaboration across teams.

These aren't just learning exercises. They're trust tests. You're showing new employees that their voice matters, that transparency is absolute, and that collaboration is how work gets done. You're also observing how they engage with your trust infrastructure.

Introduce them to your escalation paths early. Don't wait until there's a crisis to explain how to raise a concern. On day one or week one, walk new employees through your escalation and feedback mechanisms. Show them the ethics hotline, the skip-level meeting process, and the anonymous feedback tool, using whatever infrastructure you have. Explain when and how to use each one. Share stories of times when someone used these tools, and it led to positive change.

This does two things: it normalizes escalation as a routine part of how you operate, and it removes the "I didn't know how" excuse if something goes wrong later.

Procurement and Vendor Management: Trust at the Boundary

Your vendors and partners are an extension of your organization. If you're serious about trust, you can't just embed it internally; you need to extend it to your entire ecosystem. This is where many organizations fail spectacularly.

The traditional procurement process is often adversarial: get the lowest price, negotiate hard, protect yourself with contracts. This approach might save money in the short term, but it erodes trust and creates long-term risk. When your vendors don't trust you, they'll do just enough. When you don't trust them, you'll over-monitor and micromanage, wasting resources on both sides.

Here's how to redesign procurement as a trust-building system:

Start with values alignment, not just capabilities. Before you evaluate a vendor's technical capabilities or pricing, assess their values and practices. Do they treat their employees well? Do they have strong data security practices? Are they transparent about their supply chain? Do they have a track record of ethical behavior?

Create a "Trust Scorecard" (we'll detail this in the tools section) to evaluate every potential vendor. Make it clear that values alignment is a threshold requirement, not a nice-to-have. You're not just buying a service; you're entering a relationship.

Design contracts for partnership, not protection. Traditional contracts are written to protect against worst-case scenarios. They're full of penalties, termination clauses, and liability limitations. These are necessary, but they shouldn't be the dominant frame.

Add sections to your contracts that define how you'll work together: How will you communicate? How will you handle disagreements? What does success look like for both parties? How will you share information? What's your process for continuous improvement?

One manufacturing company I worked with added a "Relationship Charter" as an appendix to all its major vendor contracts. It's not legally binding, but it sets expectations for how both parties will behave. It includes commitments like "We will share relevant information proactively, not just when asked" and "We will address concerns directly with each other before escalating." It sounds soft, but it's had a measurable impact on vendor performance and relationship quality.

Build in regular trust check-ins. Don't wait for the annual review to assess how the relationship is working. Build in quarterly "relationship health" conversations that are separate from performance reviews. Use these to ask: Are we communicating effectively? Are there any concerns that haven't been addressed? What could we do differently to make this partnership more effective?

These conversations surface minor issues before they become big problems. They also reinforce that you value the relationship, not just the deliverables.

Performance Management: Where Trust Lives or Dies

Performance management is perhaps the most trust-critical system in any organization. It's where you demonstrate whether you value what you say you value. It's where people learn whether honesty is rewarded or punished. It's where trust is built or destroyed, one conversation at a time.

Traditional performance management systems, comprising annual reviews, forced rankings, and top-down feedback, destroy trust. It encourages people to hide problems, avoid risks, and focus on looking good rather than being good. We need something better.

Make Feedback Continuous and Bidirectional Replace annual reviews with ongoing conversations. Use weekly or biweekly one-on-ones not just to discuss tasks but to give and receive feedback. Make it normal for employees to provide feedback to their managers, not just the other way around.

Implement a system like "Start, Stop, Continue" in which both parties regularly share what the other should start, stop, and continue doing. This creates a rhythm of mutual accountability and improvement.

Separate Development from Compensation Decisions One of the biggest trust killers in traditional performance management is that the same conversation is supposed to cover "how are you doing?" and "how much are we paying you?" These are fundamentally different conversations that require different levels of vulnerability and honesty.

Split them. Have regular development conversations focused purely on growth, learning, and improvement. Have separate, clearly scheduled conversations about compensation. This allows people to be honest about struggles and areas for growth without fear that it will immediately impact their paycheck.

Measure what matters, including trust behaviors. If you say you value transparency, collaboration, and ethical behavior, measure them. Please include them in your performance criteria. Make it clear that how you achieve results matters as much as the results themselves.

One tech company I advised added "Trust Contribution" as a formal category in their performance reviews, weighted at 25% of the overall assessment. They defined specific behaviors: "Shares information proactively," "Raises concerns constructively," "Follows through on commitments," "Admits mistakes and learns from them." Managers had to provide specific examples for each. Within a year, they saw measurable improvements in cross-team collaboration and psychological safety scores.

Decision-Making Protocols: Transparency in Action

Every organization makes thousands of decisions every day. Most of them happen in black boxes, someone's head, a private conversation, an email thread that only a few people see. This opacity is a trust killer.

You can't make every decision transparent, but you can make your decision-making process transparent. Here's how:

Document your decision-making framework. Create a clear framework that explains how different types of decisions are made. Who has input? Who has the final say? What criteria are used? What's the timeline?

Use a model like RAPID (Recommend, Agree, Perform, Input, Decide) or DACI (Driver, Approver, Contributors, Informed) and make it standard across your organization. When someone asks, "How did we decide that?" you can point to the framework and show precisely how it was applied.

Create decision logs for significant choices. For any decision above a certain threshold of importance, create a brief decision log that captures: What was decided? Who was involved? What options were considered? What criteria were used? What was the rationale?

These logs serve multiple purposes. They create accountability. They help new people understand the context. They allow you to review past decisions and learn from them. And they demonstrate that your decision-making is principled, not arbitrary.

Build in dissent mechanisms. Make it easy and safe for people to disagree with decisions. Amazon's "disagree and commit" principle is well-known, but the key is the infrastructure that supports it. They have mechanisms for people to register their disagreement, even after a decision is formally made. This creates a record and ensures that dissenting views are heard and considered, even if they don't prevail.

Consider implementing a "Red Flag" protocol that allows anyone to raise a serious concern about a decision, triggering a mandatory review. Make it clear that raising a red flag is a valued behavior, not a career-limiting move.

Designing Ethical Escalation and Feedback Loops

Trust infrastructure isn't just about making good decisions; it's about catching and correcting bad ones. This requires robust escalation paths and feedback loops that actually work.

The Escalation Ladder: Making It Safe to Speak Up

Most organizations have some form of escalation path, an ethics hotline, an open-door policy, an HR complaint process. But having a path and having a path that people actually use are two different things.

The problem with most escalation systems is that they're designed for catastrophic failures, fraud, harassment, major ethical violations. They're not intended for everyday concerns that, if left unaddressed, eventually become disastrous.

Here's how to design an escalation system that people actually use:

Create multiple on-ramps with different levels of formality. Not every concern requires a formal investigation. Sometimes people need to talk through something with someone who can provide perspective. Sometimes they need advice on how to handle a situation. Sometimes they need to report a violation formally.

Design your escalation system with multiple entry points:

- **Informal consultation:** A trusted advisor, ombudsperson, or mentor who can provide confidential guidance without triggering a formal process.

- **Facilitated conversation:** A mediator who can help two parties work through a disagreement or concern directly.
- **Formal escalation:** A documented report that triggers investigation and action.

Make it clear when each is appropriate and how to access each. The goal is to match the response to the severity of the issue while making it easy to escalate if needed.

Guarantee protection and follow-through. The two most significant barriers to escalation are fear of retaliation and belief that nothing will change. You need to address both explicitly.

Implement strong anti-retaliation policies and enforce them visibly. When someone raises a concern, protect them. If someone retaliates, come down hard on them. Make examples (appropriately) of situations where speaking up was protected and valued.

Equally important: close the loop. When someone raises a concern, tell them what happened. You may not be able to share all details, but you can share that the matter was investigated, what general actions were taken, and what changes resulted. Nothing kills trust faster than raising a concern and hearing nothing back.

Make escalation a routine part of operations. Don't wait for problems to introduce escalation mechanisms. Build them into your regular rhythms.

One approach: implement "Pre-Mortem" sessions for major projects where teams explicitly discuss what could go wrong and how they'd raise concerns if they saw warning signs. This normalizes escalation as a planning tool rather than just a crisis response.

Another approach: include "What concerns do you have?" as a standard question in project reviews, team meetings, and one-on-ones. Make it routine to surface and discuss concerns before they become problems.

Feedback Loops: Learning from Everything

Escalation is about catching problems. Feedback loops are about learning from them. Trust-embedded organizations don't just respond to issues; they systematically learn from them and improve.

Implement "Blameless Post-Mortems" for failures. When something goes wrong, conduct a thorough review to understand what happened and how to prevent it, not to punish people.

Use a structured format:

- What happened? (Timeline of events)
- What was the impact?
- What were the contributing factors? (Technical, process, human, organizational)
- What did we learn?
- What will we change?

Share these post-mortems widely. They're some of your most valuable learning opportunities. They also demonstrate that your organization treats mistakes as learning opportunities, which encourages people to be honest when things go wrong.

Create feedback channels for your trust infrastructure itself. Your escalation paths, your decision-making processes, your policies, all of these should be subject to feedback and improvement.

Regularly ask: Are our systems working? Are there barriers to doing the right thing? Where do you see gaps between our values and our operations?

One financial services company I worked with implemented a quarterly "Trust Infrastructure Survey" in which employees rated how well various systems were working and provided suggestions for improvement. The leadership team reviews every response and publishes a summary of themes and planned actions. This creates a feedback loop on the feedback loops.

Build in leading indicators, not just lagging indicators. Most organizations measure trust outcomes, employee engagement scores, customer satisfaction, and retention rates. These are important, but they're lagging indicators. By the time they drop, you've already lost trust.

Develop leading indicators that give you early warning:

- How many concerns are being raised through your escalation channels? (More is often better, it means people trust the system)
- How long does it take to close the loop on escalated concerns?
- What percentage of decisions have documented rationale?
- How often are people using your feedback mechanisms?

- What's the trend in "trust behavior" scores in performance reviews?

Track these monthly or quarterly and treat changes as signals that require investigation.

The Trust Audit: Regular System Check-Ups

Just as you conduct financial audits and security audits, you should perform regular trust audits, systematic reviews of how well your trust infrastructure is functioning.

A trust audit examines:

- **Policy-Practice Gaps:** Where do our stated policies diverge from actual practice?
- **System Friction:** Where do our systems make trustworthy behavior difficult?
- **Blind Spots:** What risks or concerns might we be missing?
- **Effectiveness:** Are our trust mechanisms actually working?

Conduct these audits annually, or more frequently during periods of rapid change. Use a combination of data analysis (reviewing escalation patterns, decision logs, feedback themes) and qualitative research (interviews, focus groups, observation).

Most importantly: act on what you learn. An audit that doesn't lead to change is worse than no audit at all—it signals that you're going through the motions without real commitment.

Tools: Protocol Scorecard, Trust Audit Toolkit

Let's get tactical. Here are two concrete tools you can implement immediately to start embedding trust into your infrastructure.

Tool #1: The Protocol Scorecard

The Protocol Scorecard is a framework for evaluating any process, policy, or system against trust principles. Use it when designing new systems or auditing existing ones.

How to Use It

For any process or system, rate it on a scale of 1–5 (1 = significant gap, 5 = exemplary) across these dimensions:

1. Transparency:

- Are the rules and criteria clear and accessible?
- Can people see how decisions are made?
- Is information shared proactively?

Example questions to ask:

- If I'm new to the organization, can I understand how this works without asking someone?
- Are the decision criteria documented and available?
- Do people know where to find information about this process?

2. Accessibility:

- Is it easy to engage with this system?
- Are there barriers (time, complexity, fear) that prevent people from using it?
- Does it work for everyone, or only for those with certain knowledge/access?

Example questions to ask:

- How many steps does it take to complete this process?
- What happens if someone doesn't follow the process perfectly?
- Can someone use this system without special knowledge or connections?

3. Consistency:

- Does this system produce similar outcomes for similar inputs?
- Are there hidden variables (who you know, timing, luck) that significantly impact outcomes?
- Can people predict what will happen if they engage with this system?

Example questions to ask:

- If two people in similar situations use this system, will they get similar results?

- Are there documented exceptions, or do exceptions happen ad hoc?
- Can we explain variations in outcomes?

4. Accountability

- Is it clear who owns this system and who's responsible for outcomes?
- Are there mechanisms to review and improve the system?
- What happens when the system fails or produces bad outcomes?

Example questions to ask:

- Who do I talk to if this system isn't working?
- How do we know if this system is achieving its goals?
- What's our process for updating this system based on feedback?

5. Learning:

- Does this system help us get better over time?
- Do we capture and act on feedback?
- When things go wrong, do we understand why and improve?

Example questions to ask:

- How do we collect feedback on this system?
- When was the last time we updated this process based on what we learned?
- Do we have data on how well this system is working?

6. Values Alignment:

- Does this system make it easier to live up to our stated values?
- Are there conflicts between what this system rewards and what we say we value?
- Does using this system feel consistent with our organizational identity?

Example questions to ask:

- If we say we value X, does this system support or undermine that?

- What behaviors does this system actually reward?
- Would we be proud to explain this system to a new employee or customer?

Scoring and Action:

- **Total Score 25–30:** This system is a trusted asset. Document what's working and consider it a model for other systems.
- **Total Score 18–24:** This system is functional but has room for improvement. Prioritize the lowest-scoring dimensions for enhancement.
- **Total Score 12–17:** This system has significant trust gaps. Conduct a deeper review and develop a remediation plan.
- **Total Score 6–11:** This system is actively undermining trust. Consider whether to redesign it completely or eliminate it.

Implementation Example

Let's apply this to a standard system: expense reimbursement.

Transparency (3/5) The policy is documented, but it's 15 pages long and uses accounting jargon. Most people learn the fundamental rules from colleagues, not the policy.

Accessibility (2/5) The system requires scanning receipts, completing a form with multiple fields, obtaining manager approval, and waiting 2–3 weeks for reimbursement. Many employees eat small expenses rather than deal with the hassle.

Consistency (4/5) The system generally produces consistent outcomes, though rumors suggest some managers are more lenient than others.

Accountability (3/5) It's clear who processes expenses, but there's no clear path to appeal a rejection or suggest improvements to the system.

Learning (2/5) The system hasn't been updated in five years despite regular complaints about its complexity.

Values Alignment (2/5) The company says it values employee wellbeing and trust, but the system treats employees as potential fraudsters who need extensive oversight.

Total Score: 16/30—Significant trust gaps.

Action Plan:

1. Simplify the policy to one page of clear guidelines with examples
2. Implement auto-approval for expenses under $50
3. Reduce reimbursement time to 3–5 business days
4. Create a quarterly review process for the expense system
5. Add a "suggest improvement" button to the expense submission form

Tool #2: The Trust Audit Toolkit

The Trust Audit Toolkit is a comprehensive framework for conducting a systematic review of your organization's trust infrastructure. Use it annually or when you're experiencing trust issues.

Phase 1: Data Collection

Gather quantitative and qualitative data across these categories:

A. System Usage Data:

- How many people are using your escalation channels? (Track over time)
- What's the average time to resolve escalated concerns?
- How many decisions have a documented rationale?
- What's the completion rate for feedback surveys?
- What are the trends in employee engagement and trust scores?

B. Process Review:

- Map your key processes (onboarding, performance management, decision-making, procurement, etc.)
- For each process, run it through the Protocol Scorecard
- Identify the lowest-scoring processes for deeper investigation

C. Stakeholder Interviews:

Conduct confidential interviews with a representative sample of employees at all levels. Ask:

- "Describe a time when you needed to raise a concern. What happened?"
- "When you see a decision being made, do you understand how and why? Can you give an example?"
- "Are there situations where you feel pressure to cut corners or compromise on values? What creates that pressure?"
- "What systems or processes make it easy to do the right thing? Which makes it hard?"
- "If you could change one thing about how we operate to increase trust, what would it be?"

D. Incident Analysis:

Review all escalated concerns, ethics reports, and significant failures from the past year:

- What patterns emerge?
- Were there early warning signs that were missed?
- How effective were our responses?
- What did we learn and change as a result?

Phase 2: Analysis

Synthesize your data to identify:

Trust Assets: Systems and practices that are working well and building trust. Document these as models.

Trust Gaps: Areas where there's a significant gap between stated values and operational reality. Prioritize these for action.

Trust Risks: Situations or systems that could lead to trust failures if not addressed. These may not be problems yet, but they're vulnerabilities.

Trust Opportunities: Areas where relatively minor changes could significantly improve trust. These are your quick wins.

Create a visual "Trust Infrastructure Map" that shows:

- Which systems are trust assets (green)
- Which have moderate gaps (yellow)

- Which have significant gaps (red)
- Which are trust risks (orange)

This gives you a clear picture of where you stand and where to focus.

Phase 3: Action Planning

For each identified gap or risk, develop a specific action plan:

What: What exactly will we change?
Why: What trust principle does this address?
Who: Who owns this change?
When: What's the timeline?
How: What resources are needed?
Measure: How will we know if it's working?

Prioritize based on:

- **Impact:** How much will this improve trust?
- **Feasibility:** How easy is this to implement?
- **Urgency:** How risky is it to delay?

Focus on a mix of quick wins (high impact, high feasibility) and strategic investments (high impact, lower feasibility but essential for long-term trust).

Phase 4: Implementation and Monitoring

Execute your action plan with these principles:

Communicate transparently: Share what you learned from the audit and what you're changing. Be honest about gaps and limitations.

Start with visible changes: Choose some early actions that people will notice. This builds credibility for the broader effort.

Close the loop: As you implement changes, let people know. Show them that the audit led to real improvements.

Monitor leading indicators: Track whether your changes are having the intended effect. Are more people using escalation channels? Are decision logs being created? Are trust scores improving?

Iterate: Treat this as an ongoing process, not a one-time project. Plan your next audit and continue refining.

Implementation Example

A mid-sized healthcare organization conducted a trust audit and discovered:

Trust Assets: Their patient safety reporting system was highly trusted and well-used. Their onboarding program effectively communicated values.
Trust Gaps: Their performance review system was opaque and inconsistent. Their procurement process was slow and frustrating, leading to workarounds.
Trust Risks: They had no clear escalation path for concerns about leadership behavior. Their decision-making about resource allocation was seen as political rather than principled.
Trust Opportunities: Small changes to meeting practices (sharing agendas in advance, documenting decisions) could significantly improve transparency.

Action Plan:

1. **Immediate** (0–3 months): Implement meeting documentation standards, create leadership escalation path, simplify procurement for purchases under $5K
2. **Near-term** (3–6 months): Redesign performance review system with clear criteria and calibration process
3. **Strategic** (6–12 months): Develop and communicate a resource allocation framework, train all managers on trust-building practices

They assigned owners to each initiative, set up monthly check-ins to monitor progress, and committed to sharing updates quarterly with the whole organization.

Six months later, their employee engagement scores had improved by 12 points, and voluntary turnover had decreased by 30%. More importantly, they'd created a foundation of trust infrastructure that would continue to pay dividends.

Conclusion: From Infrastructure to Culture

Here's what we've learned in this chapter: trust isn't just a feeling or a cultural aspiration. It's an operational reality that must be embedded in your organization's systems, processes, and infrastructure. Its code needs to be written, debugged, and continuously improved.

When you design your onboarding to teach not just what to do but how decisions get made, you're writing trust into your foundation. When you create procurement processes that prioritize value alignment alongside cost and capability, you're building trust within your ecosystem. When you build performance management systems that separate development from compensation and measure trust behaviors, you're making trust a competitive advantage. When you design escalation paths that are actually used and feedback loops that actually lead to change, you're creating an organization that learns and improves.

This is hard work. It requires you to examine every process, every policy, every system through the lens of trust. It requires you to close the gaps between what you say you value and what your systems actually reward. It requires you to make trustworthy behavior the path of least resistance, not the heroic exception.

But it's worth it. Because organizations with strong trust infrastructure don't just avoid catastrophic failures, though they do that, they move faster, because people don't need to verify and double-check constantly. They innovate more because people feel safe experimenting and sharing ideas. They attract and retain better talent, because people want to work in environments where trust is absolute, not just rhetoric. They build stronger relationships with customers, partners, and communities because their trustworthiness is evident in how they operate, not just what they claim.

The tools we've covered in this chapter, the Protocol Scorecard and the Trust Audit Toolkit, give you concrete ways to start this work. Use them. Adapt them to your context. Please share them with your teams. Make trust infrastructure a regular topic of conversation in your leadership meetings.

In the previous chapters, we've built the foundation: understanding trust as a strategic asset, exploring how trust forms in the brain, examining leadership's role in modeling trust, learning how to build trust across teams, and developing the skills to repair trust when it breaks. Now we've added the operational layer, the systems and infrastructure that make trust sustainable at scale.

In the next chapter, we'll explore how to measure trust and demonstrate its impact on business outcomes. Because if you can't measure it, you can't manage it, and you certainly can't make the case for continued investment in trust infrastructure. We'll examine the metrics that matter, the data you need to collect, and how to build a compelling business case for trust as a strategic priority.

But for now, start where you are. Pick one system: maybe onboarding, maybe procurement, maybe performance management. Run it through the Protocol Scorecard. Identify the gaps. Plan to close them. Write trust into that one system and then move to the next.

Because trust as code isn't built overnight. It's built one system, one process, one decision at a time. And every line of code you write makes your organization stronger, more resilient, and more trustworthy.

The infrastructure you build today will determine the trust you have tomorrow. So start building.

7
Leading in the Age of AI, Automation, and Ethics

The Black Box at 10,000 Feet

Faced with conflicting information from sources, it was clear he could not see inside the system and felt a realization settle in. It was a realization that would fundamentally reshape his, and my, understanding of leadership. We were already living in the age of algorithmic decision making, and most people had no idea how to lead through it.

From the cockpit, the terrain below shifted in the green glow of the night vision display. Forty minutes into a mission in Afghanistan, the crew was providing communications support for a reconnaissance operation when the aircraft's automated threat detection system lit up. Its warning tone was sharp and unmistakable, familiar from training but never before heard in combat.

The pilot's voice crackled through the intercom: "We've got a possible threat. System says it's tracking us."

In that moment, when the pilot looked back, the question hit; do we trust the system or our team on the ground?Across the console, the communications specialist scanned the screen. The encrypted data feed from ground units showed no unusual activity. Yet the aircraft's defensive suite, a tightly integrated network of sensors and algorithms he had helped bring online even if its inner workings defied simple explanation, was signaling danger. The human intelligence on the ground was signaling something else entirely.

We trusted our team and the reporting coming in from humans over the technology that day. The system had generated a false positive; a flock of birds had triggered the threat detection algorithm in a way the programmers hadn't anticipated. We completed the mission safely, but I couldn't stop thinking about that moment. What if we'd been wrong? What if next time the algorithm was correct and we ignored it?

DOI: 10.1201/9781003688815-8

Fifteen years later, I watch business leaders face the same dilemma every day. They're not flying over Afghanistan, but they're making decisions based on AI systems they don't understand, algorithms they can't see inside, and automated processes that increasingly shape their organizations. The stakes might not be life and death, but they're real: careers, livelihoods, company survival, and the trust of everyone who depends on them.

This chapter is about leading when you can't see inside the black box. It's about building trust in an age when the systems we rely on are increasingly opaque, when automation makes decisions faster than we can think, and when the ethical implications of our technological choices ripple out in ways we're only beginning to understand.

Trusting Systems We Can't See

In Afghanistan, I worked with systems I couldn't fully comprehend. I knew the basics, how to configure them, how to troubleshoot common problems, and how to read the outputs. But the actual algorithms running inside encrypted communications systems, the threat-detection software, and the automated network routing protocols? Those were black boxes to me.

Yet I had to trust them. More importantly, I had to help others trust them.

This is the fundamental challenge of leadership in the age of AI and automation. You're responsible for decisions made by systems you don't, and often can't, fully understand. You're accountable for outcomes generated by algorithms that even their creators sometimes struggle to explain.

The temptation is to retreat into one of two extremes. The first is blind faith: "The AI said it, so it must be right." I've seen this in military contexts and business environments alike. Leaders who relinquish their judgment to the algorithm, who stop asking critical questions because the system seems so sophisticated, so confident in its outputs.

The second extreme is complete rejection: "I don't trust anything I can't understand." These leaders resist automation entirely, insisting on manual processes and human decision-making for everything. They fall behind, unable to compete with organizations that have learned to leverage these tools effectively.

Neither approach builds trust. Neither approach works.

The path forward requires what I call "informed trust," a middle ground where you don't need to understand every line of code, but you do need to understand the system's logic, its limitations, its failure modes, and its track record.

Think about how we approached communications security in the military. I didn't need to understand the mathematical foundations of encryption algorithms. But I did need to know:

- What the system was designed to do and what it wasn't
- How it had performed in similar conditions
- What could cause it to fail or produce unreliable outputs
- How to verify its outputs against other sources
- When to escalate concerns to someone with more profound expertise

This same framework applies to AI systems in business. When your company implements an AI-powered hiring tool, you don't need a PhD in machine learning. But you do need to ask:

What is this system optimizing for? Is it screening for skills, cultural fit, or something else entirely? Many AI hiring tools optimize for "similarity to successful employees," which sounds reasonable until you realize it can perpetuate existing biases and create homogeneous teams.

How was it trained? What data did it learn from? If your AI was trained on historical hiring data from a company with diversity problems, it will likely recommend candidates who perpetuate those problems.

What are its known failure modes? Every system has edge cases where it performs poorly. A facial recognition system might struggle with certain lighting conditions. A natural language processing tool might misinterpret industry-specific jargon. Know where your systems are weakest.

How do we verify its outputs? In Afghanistan, we never relied on a single source of intelligence. We cross-referenced automated systems with human observation, multiple sensors, and historical patterns. The same principle applies to business AI. If your algorithm recommends firing a high performer, you'd better have human judgment and additional data points in the mix.

I learned this lesson through multiple deployments to Afghanistan. Units implemented automated systems for prioritizing communications traffic. Essentially, an algorithm that decided which messages got through first when bandwidth was limited. It worked beautifully for weeks, efficiently routing routine traffic and prioritizing urgent communications.

Then one day, it deprioritized a message that turned out to be critical. The algorithm had classified it as routine based on specific keywords and metadata, but the content was actually time-sensitive intelligence. No one was hurt, but the delay could have had serious consequences.

The problem wasn't the algorithm itself. The problem was that we'd started trusting it implicitly. We'd stopped spot-checking its decisions. We'd stopped asking, "Does this make sense?" We'd let efficiency override judgment.

After that incident, we implemented what I now call "trust verification protocols." We didn't abandon the automated system; it was still valuable, but we added human checkpoints. Certain types of messages always got a human review, regardless of what the algorithm recommended. We tracked the algorithm's decisions and regularly audited them for patterns that might indicate problems. We created a feedback loop so that when the algorithm made a mistake, we could understand why and improve it.

This is the model for leading with AI and automation. You're not choosing between human and machine. You're architecting a system where both contribute their strengths and compensate for each other's weaknesses.

The trust you're building isn't just trust in the technology. It's trust in your judgment about when to rely on the technology, when to question it, and when to override it. Your team needs to trust that you won't unreservedly follow an algorithm off a cliff, but they also need to trust that you won't reject valuable insights just because they came from a machine.

This requires transparency about what you know and what you don't. In military briefings, we used confidence levels such as "We assess with high confidence," or "We have low confidence in." Business leaders need the same honesty about AI outputs. "The algorithm recommends this, and based on its track record in similar situations, I'm confident in that recommendation" is very different from "The algorithm recommends this, and I don't fully understand why, but let's proceed anyway."

The systems we can't see inside are only going to become more prevalent. The leaders who thrive won't be those who understand every technical detail. There will be those who know how to build appropriate trust frameworks around opaque systems. Trust that's neither blind nor cynical, but informed, verified, and constantly calibrated.

Algorithmic Fairness, Bias, and Explainers

During my time working with reconnaissance units, I saw firsthand how bias could creep into even the most sophisticated automated systems. We had pattern-of-life analysis tools, algorithms that analyzed surveillance data and flagged unusual behavior that might indicate threats. These systems were remarkably effective, but they had a dangerous flaw: they were only as good as their training data and the assumptions baked into their design.

I remember reviewing flagged incidents with an intelligence analyst who'd spent years in the region. The algorithm had identified several "suspicious" movement patterns in a particular village. But the analyst immediately recognized what the algorithm had missed: it was a market day, and the "unusual" activity was entirely regular in that context. The algorithm had been trained primarily on data from urban areas and didn't account for rural market patterns.

The system wasn't broken. It wasn't very objective. And that bias could have led to catastrophic decisions.

This is the uncomfortable truth about AI and automation: they don't eliminate human bias. They encode it, scale it, and give it the veneer of objectivity. An algorithm doesn't feel prejudiced. It doesn't have malicious intent. But it can absolutely perpetuate and amplify the biases present in its training data, its design, or the objectives it's been given.

As a leader, you need to understand that "the algorithm decided" is not a shield against bias. It's often a magnifier of it.

Consider a real-world example: Amazon developed an AI recruiting tool trained on 10 years of hiring data. The algorithm learned to penalize resumes that included the word "women's," as in "women's chess club captain." Why? Because historical data showed that Amazon had hired more men than women, the algorithm was optimized to match successful past hires. Amazon scrapped the tool, but how many companies are using similar systems without realizing the bias baked in?

Or consider predictive policing algorithms that recommend where to deploy officers based on historical crime data. Sounds reasonable, except that historical data reflects where police have been deployed in the past, which often reflects historical biases about which neighborhoods are "high crime." The algorithm creates a feedback loop: police are sent to specific neighborhoods, find more crime there (because they're looking), which reinforces the algorithm's recommendation to send more police there.

The military concept of "ground truth" is essential here. In intelligence analysis, ground truth means verifying algorithmic outputs against direct observation and diverse sources. You don't just trust the sensor data; you send someone to look for themselves. You don't just trust one perspective; you seek multiple viewpoints.

Business leaders need the same discipline. When your AI system makes a recommendation, ask:

Who is represented in the training data, and who isn't? If your customer service AI was trained primarily on interactions with a single demographic, it may perform poorly with other demographics. If your credit risk algorithm learned from historical lending data that reflected discriminatory practices, it will perpetuate those practices.

What is the algorithm optimizing for, and what might it be sacrificing? An algorithm optimizing for efficiency might sacrifice fairness. One might optimize for accuracy at the expense of coverage. One who optimizes for engagement might sacrifice user well-being. You need to know the tradeoffs.

Who designed this system, and what assumptions did they bring? Homogeneous teams build homogeneous systems. If your AI development team doesn't include diverse perspectives, they're likely to miss edge cases and failure modes that would be obvious to someone with different experiences.

Can the system explain its decisions? This is where "explainable AI" becomes critical. In military intelligence, we didn't just want to know what the system concluded; we wanted to know why. What data points led to this assessment? What patterns did it identify? What confidence level should we assign?

The same principle applies to business AI. If your algorithm denies someone a loan, promotes one employee over another, or recommends firing someone, you need to be able to explain why. Not just "the algorithm said so," but what factors the algorithm weighted and how it reached that conclusion.

This isn't just about fairness, though that's reason enough. It's about trust. When people understand how decisions are made, they're more likely to trust the process even if they disagree with the outcome. When decisions emerge from an opaque black box, trust erodes quickly.

I've seen leaders try to hide behind algorithmic opacity. "I can't explain why the system made that decision; it's too complex." That's not leadership. That's abdication. If you can't explain it, you shouldn't be implementing it.

Some of the most effective tools I've encountered are "bias audits," systematic reviews of AI systems to identify potential fairness issues. These audits ask questions like:

- Does the system perform equally well across different demographic groups?
- Are there patterns in who benefits and who is harmed by the system's decisions?
- What happens in edge cases or with unusual inputs?
- How does the system handle missing or incomplete data?
- What feedback mechanisms exist to identify and correct bias?

In Afghanistan, we conducted regular "red team" exercises in which people actively sought flaws in our systems. We didn't wait for failures to happen in the field; we proactively stress-tested our assumptions. Business leaders should do the same with their AI systems.

Create a "bias red team" whose job is to identify potential fairness issues before they cause harm. Include people with diverse backgrounds and perspectives. Give them permission to challenge assumptions and ask uncomfortable questions. Make it safe to identify problems rather than hiding them.

One practical tool I recommend is the "Bias Impact Statement." Before deploying any AI system that affects people: hiring, promotion, customer service, credit decisions, whatever. Require a written statement that addresses:

1. What populations might be affected differently by this system?
2. What steps have been taken to identify and mitigate bias?
3. How will we monitor for bias after deployment?
4. What's our plan if we discover bias we didn't anticipate?

This isn't bureaucracy for its own sake. It's forcing the hard conversations before you've committed to a system, before you've harmed people, before you've damaged trust.

The goal isn't to achieve perfect fairness, that's often impossible, and different people have different definitions of what "fair" even means. The goal is to make conscious, informed choices about tradeoffs, to be transparent about those choices, and to monitor and adjust as you learn more continuously.

In the military, we accepted that our systems would never be perfect. But we insisted they be accountable. The same standard should apply to business AI. Your algorithms don't need to be flawless, but they do need to be explainable, auditable, and improvable.

The leaders who build trust in the age of AI won't be those who deploy the most sophisticated algorithms. There will be those who deploy algorithms responsibly, understand their limitations, actively work to identify and mitigate bias, and can explain their systems' decisions in terms humans can understand and evaluate.

Human Oversight in Automated Environments

There's a concept in military aviation called "automation complacency." It happens when pilots become so reliant on automated systems that their skills degrade and their situational awareness diminishes. They stop actively flying the aircraft and start passively monitoring the automation. Everything works fine until it doesn't, and then they're not prepared to take over.

The most famous example is Air France Flight 447, which crashed into the Atlantic Ocean in 2009, killing all 228 people aboard. The autopilot disconnected due to iced-over sensors, and the pilots, who had become so accustomed to automated flight, made a series of errors that led to the crash. The investigation revealed that the pilots had lost basic manual flying skills because they so rarely needed them.

This is the dark side of automation: it can make us less capable even as it makes our systems more capable.

I envision a version of this in Afghanistan with our communications networks. We'd implement sophisticated automated routing protocols that handled most network management tasks without human intervention. The systems would be excellent; they optimize bandwidth, reroute around failures, and generally keep everything running smoothly.

But then think of something troubling: the junior soldiers who'd joined after we implemented these systems didn't develop the same deep understanding of network architecture as earlier generations. Why would they? The automation handled everything. They knew how to monitor the systems and respond to alerts, but they didn't really understand what was happening under the hood.

This becomes a problem when remove faced with a scenario that the automation wasn't designed for. An adversary was using a jamming technique that our automated systems couldn't effectively counter. The systems kept trying the exact solutions, failing, and trying again. We needed human creativity and deep technical knowledge to develop a workaround.

The senior soldiers who'd learned networking before the automation could do it. The junior soldiers, despite being technically proficient with the automated tools, struggled. The automation had made them efficient but not expert.

This is the central challenge of human oversight in automated environments: how do you maintain human expertise and judgment when automation handles most routine tasks? How do you keep people engaged and capable when their primary role is monitoring systems rather than actively doing the work?

The answer isn't to eliminate automation; that ship has sailed, and automation provides real value. The answer is to architect human oversight deliberately and thoughtfully.

In military operations, we use concepts like "human in the loop," "human on the loop," and "human out of the loop" to describe different levels of automation:

Human-in-the-loop means a human must approve each decision before it's executed. The system can recommend, but it can't act without human authorization. This is appropriate for high-stakes, irreversible decisions. In the military, weapons systems that target humans typically require human approval. In business, decisions like firing employees or denying critical benefits should probably require human approval.

Human-on-the-loop means the system can act autonomously, with a human monitoring and intervening if needed. This is appropriate for routine decisions where speed matters but human judgment is still valuable. Think of an AI customer service system that handles most inquiries automatically but flags complex or sensitive issues for human review.

Human out-of-the-loop means the system operates entirely autonomously. This is appropriate only for low-stakes, easily reversible decisions where human oversight adds little value. Maybe automated email sorting or routine data backups.

The key is matching the level of automation to the stakes and reversibility of the decision. Too much human involvement unnecessarily slows things down. Too little human involvement creates risk and erodes expertise.

But here's what many leaders miss: even with human oversight, you need to design it carefully to avoid the illusion of oversight. Research shows that humans monitoring automated systems often miss errors because they're not actively engaged. They're passively watching, assuming the system is working correctly, and their attention drifts.

In aviation, this is addressed through "active monitoring" protocols. Pilots are trained to continuously cross-check automated systems against other instruments, to verbalize what they're seeing, and to practice manual flying skills even when automation is available regularly. They don't just watch the autopilot; they actively verify it's doing what it should.

Business leaders need similar protocols. If you have humans "overseeing" an AI system, what does that oversight actually entail? Are they:

- Actively reviewing a sample of decisions to verify quality?
- Checking the system's outputs against other data sources?
- Looking for patterns that might indicate problems?
- Maintaining their own expertise so they can recognize when something is wrong?

Or are they just watching a dashboard turn green and assuming everything is fine?

I recommend what I call "active oversight protocols" for any significant automated system:

Regular sampling and review. Don't just review flagged issues; randomly sample routine decisions to verify the system is working as intended. In Afghanistan, we didn't just investigate communications failures; we regularly audited successful transmissions to ensure our systems were performing correctly.

Skill maintenance requirements. People overseeing automated systems should regularly practice doing the task manually. If your AI handles customer service, your human overseers should regularly handle customer inquiries themselves. If your algorithm screens resumes, your recruiters should screen resumes manually regularly. This keeps their skills sharp and their judgment calibrated.

Escalation protocols. Define clear criteria for when humans should intervene. Don't make it subjective ("intervene when something seems wrong"). Make it specific: "Intervene when the confidence score is below X, when the decision affects more than Y people, when the outcome is irreversible," etc.

Feedback loops. Create mechanisms for humans to flag issues and improve the system. In the military, we had "after-action reviews" to analyze what went right and what went wrong. Your automated systems need the same. When a human overrides the AI, capture why. When the AI makes a mistake, understand what led to it. Use this information to improve both the system and the oversight protocols.

Diverse oversight. Don't rely on a single person or perspective to oversee automated systems. Different people will notice different problems. In intelligence analysis, we used "red teams" and "blue teams" to challenge each other's assumptions. Your AI oversight should include multiple perspectives.

One of the most essential lessons from military operations is the concept of "commander's intent." Even when we used sophisticated automated systems, we always maintained clarity about the ultimate objective and the values guiding our decisions. The automation was a tool to achieve the intent, not a replacement for it.

Business leaders need the same clarity. What is your organization trying to achieve? What values guide your decisions? When you implement automation, are you clear about how it serves those objectives and upholds those values?

I've seen too many organizations implement AI systems without this clarity. They automate because they can. After all, it's efficient, because everyone else is doing it. But they haven't thought through whether the automation actually serves their mission or might undermine it.

Ask yourself: If this automated system makes a technically optimal decision that feels wrong, what happens? Do your people have permission to override it? Do they have the expertise to recognize when they should? Do they understand the values that should guide that judgment?

The future isn't humans or machines. It's humans and machines, working together, with clear roles and clear accountability. The leaders who get this right will build systems where automation handles what it does best: speed, consistency, and processing vast amounts of data. While humans contribute what they do best: judgment, creativity, ethical reasoning, and contextual understanding.

But this only works if you actively maintain human capability and engagement. Automation complacency isn't just a risk in aviation. It's a risk in every automated environment. The antidote is deliberate, thoughtful, active human oversight, not as an afterthought, but as a core design principle.

Tools: Future Risk Matrix and AI Trust Framework

Theory is valuable, but leaders need practical tools. Here are two frameworks I've developed to help leaders navigate AI, automation, and ethics in their organizations.

The Future Risk Matrix

When evaluating whether to implement an AI or automation system, leaders often focus on the potential benefits while underestimating the risks. The Future Risk Matrix helps you systematically assess risks across four critical dimensions:

1. Transparency Risk:

- **High Risk:** The system is a complete black box. Even experts can't explain how it reaches decisions. You can't audit its logic or understand its failure modes.
- **Medium Risk:** The system can provide some explanation of its decisions, but only in technical terms that most stakeholders won't understand. Auditing is possible but difficult.
- **Low Risk:** The system can explain its decisions in plain language. Its logic is auditable and understandable to non-technical stakeholders.

Questions to ask:

- Can we explain to affected parties how decisions are made?
- Can we audit the system's logic if problems arise?
- Do we understand the system well enough to identify when it's wrong?

2. Reversibility Risk:

- **High Risk:** Decisions are difficult or impossible to reverse. Once made, they create lasting consequences.
- **Medium Risk:** Decisions can be reversed, but only with significant effort, cost, or disruption.
- **Low Risk:** Decisions are easily reversible with minimal consequences.

Questions to ask:

- If the system makes a mistake, how hard is it to fix?
- What's the cost, financial, reputational, human, of reversing a decision?
- Can we implement a "trial period" where decisions are easily undone?

3. Impact Risk

- **High Risk:** Decisions significantly affect people's lives, livelihoods, safety, or fundamental rights.
- **Medium Risk:** Decisions affect people's experience or opportunities but aren't life-altering.
- **Low Risk:** Decisions have minimal impact on individuals.

Questions to ask:

- Who is affected by this system's decisions?
- What's the worst-case scenario if it makes a mistake?
- Are we making decisions about people's access to essential resources or opportunities?

4. Bias Risk:

- **High Risk:** The system makes decisions about diverse populations but was trained on limited or biased data. No bias testing has been conducted.
- **Medium Risk:** Some bias testing has been conducted, but gaps remain. Monitoring is limited.
- **Low Risk:** Comprehensive bias testing has been conducted across relevant populations. Ongoing monitoring is in place.

Questions to ask:

- How diverse was the training data?
- Have we tested for differential performance across demographic groups?
- Do we have mechanisms to detect and correct bias after deployment?

Using the Matrix

Plot your AI system across these four dimensions. Systems that score high risk on multiple dimensions require the most stringent oversight and may not be appropriate for deployment at all. Systems that score low risk across all dimensions can operate with lighter oversight.

For example:

- An AI that recommends Netflix shows: Low transparency risk (you can see why it recommends things), low reversibility risk (you can ignore recommendations), low impact risk (it's just entertainment), low bias risk (the stakes are minimal). This can operate with minimal oversight.

- An AI that screens job applicants: Medium-to-high transparency risk (depending on the system), medium reversibility risk (you can interview people the AI rejected, but you probably won't), high impact risk (affects people's livelihoods), high bias risk (well-documented issues with hiring AI). This requires significant human oversight and bias testing.
- An AI that determines prison sentences: High risk across all dimensions. This probably shouldn't exist without extensive safeguards, if at all.

The AI Trust Framework

This is a practical checklist for evaluating whether an AI system is trustworthy. Before deploying any AI system, work through these questions with your team:

Authentication: Do we know what this system is and where it came from?

- We understand who developed this system and their track record
- We know what data the system was trained on
- We understand the system's intended use case and limitations
- We have documentation of the system's development and testing
- We know what version we're using and how it's been updated

Authorization: Is this system appropriate for this use case?

- The system's capabilities match our needs
- The system has been validated for our specific context
- We've defined clear boundaries for what the system should and shouldn't do
- We've identified decisions that require human approval
- We have appropriate legal and ethical authorization to use this system

Encryption: Is the system secure and private?

- Sensitive data is protected appropriately
- We understand what data the system collects and how it's used
- We've assessed cybersecurity risks
- We comply with relevant privacy regulations
- We have protocols for data breaches or security incidents

Resilience: Can we handle failures and adapt to them?

- We've identified potential failure modes
- We have monitoring systems to detect problems
- We have protocols for human intervention when needed
- We have a plan for system failures or outages
- We have mechanisms to improve the system based on feedback

Explainability: Can we understand and explain decisions?

- The system can provide explanations for its decisions
- Explanations are understandable to relevant stakeholders
- We can audit the system's decision-making process
- We can identify why the system made mistakes
- We can explain the system's logic to affected parties

Fairness: Does the system treat people equitably?

- We've tested for bias across relevant demographic groups
- We've identified potential fairness issues and mitigation strategies
- We have ongoing monitoring for bias
- We have processes to address fairness complaints
- We've considered different definitions of fairness and made conscious choices

Accountability: Do we know who's responsible?

- We've clearly assigned responsibility for the system's decisions
- We have processes for addressing mistakes or harm
- We have mechanisms for affected parties to appeal decisions
- We've defined consequences for system failures
- We have clear escalation paths for problems

Human Oversight: Are humans appropriately involved?

- We've determined the appropriate level of human involvement (in/on/out of loop)
- Humans overseeing the system have appropriate expertise
- We have protocols for maintaining human skills and judgment
- We've defined clear criteria for human intervention
- We have processes for humans to override the system when needed

Impact Assessment: Do we understand the consequences?

- We've identified who is affected by this system
- We've assessed potential harms and benefits
- We've considered unintended consequences
- We've evaluated whether benefits justify risks
- We have plans to mitigate adverse impacts

Continuous Improvement: Are we learning and adapting?

- We have mechanisms to collect feedback on system performance
- We regularly review and audit the system
- We have processes to update the system based on learnings
- We track metrics on system performance and fairness
- We have a plan for decommissioning the system if needed

Using the Framework

This isn't a one-time checklist. It's an ongoing protocol. Before deployment, work through every item. If you can't check a box, that's a gap you need to address. After deployment, regularly revisit the framework to ensure your systems remain trustworthy as they evolve and as your understanding deepens.

I recommend quarterly reviews for high-risk systems and annual reviews for medium-risk systems. Assign someone to own this process; do not let it become everyone's responsibility, and therefore no one's responsibility.

The age of AI and automation isn't coming. It's here. The question isn't whether you'll lead in this environment, but how you'll lead. Will you lead with blind faith in technology, abdicating your judgment to algorithms? Will you lead with fearful resistance, rejecting valuable tools because you don't understand them? Or will you lead with informed trust, leveraging automation's strengths while maintaining human judgment, expertise, and ethical oversight?

The leaders who thrive will be those who recognize that AI and automation aren't just technical challenges. They're trust challenges. Every automated system you deploy is a statement about what you value, who you trust, and how you make decisions. Your people are watching. Your customers are watching. The communities you affect are watching.

They're not asking whether you use AI. They're asking whether you use it responsibly, whether you can explain it, whether you've thought through the consequences, and whether you maintain the human judgment and values that technology alone can never provide.

In that helicopter over Afghanistan, staring at conflicting information from systems we couldn't see inside, we learned that leadership in the age of automation isn't about choosing between human and machine. It's about architecting systems where both contribute their strengths, where trust is earned through transparency and verification, and where humans remain accountable for the decisions that matter most.

That lesson has never been more relevant than it is today. The systems are more sophisticated, the stakes are higher, and the need for thoughtful, ethical leadership is greater than ever. The tools in this chapter can help, but the choice is yours: What kind of leader will you be in the age of AI?

Conclusion

You Are the Protocol

I still remember that turn.

Late at night, somewhere between North Carolina and New York City, my GPS told me to turn left. Everything in my gut said it was wrong. The road looked abandoned. The darkness felt absolute. I had trusted that system a hundred times before and verified its authentication. I had tested its resilience. I had encrypted my route into its memory and arrived safely time and time again.

But what if I turned left?

The GPS wasn't right; my instincts were. And in that moment, I understood something that would take me years to articulate: trust isn't about suppressing doubt. It's about building systems so robust that doubt becomes irrelevant.

That's what this book is about. Not trust as a feeling. Not trust as a personality trait. Not trust as something you inspire through charisma or manufacture through motivation. Trust as infrastructure. Trust as protocol. Trust is the hardened, tested, resilient system that keeps organizations operational when everything else fails.

You've learned the frameworks. You've seen the tools. You've mapped the vulnerabilities and designed the response protocols. You've studied authentication, encryption, and resilience. You've built human firewalls and embedded trust as code. You've prepared for the automation age, where trust must scale beyond human capacity.

Now comes the most challenging part: implementation.

Not someday. Not when conditions are perfect. Not when you have more resources, better people, or more explicit mandates.

Now.

Because here's what I learned in Afghanistan that applies to every boardroom, every team meeting, every organizational crisis you'll face:

DOI: 10.1201/9781003688815-9

the protocol doesn't wait for perfect conditions. The protocol *creates* the conditions. And you, the leader reading this, you are the protocol.

Daily Trust Rituals: The Operational Discipline of Leadership

Let me be direct: everything you've read means nothing without daily practice. Trust infrastructure doesn't build itself. It requires the same operational discipline as any other critical system. You wouldn't skip daily security patches because you didn't feel like it. You wouldn't ignore firewall logs because you were busy. You wouldn't defer authentication protocols because they seemed tedious.

Trust requires the same rigor.

Here are the non-negotiable daily rituals that separate leaders who build trust infrastructure from leaders who merely talk about it:

The Morning Authentication Check (10 minutes)

Before you check your email. Before you review your calendar. Before you do anything else, you run your authentication audit. Ask yourself three questions:

1. What credibility did I build yesterday? (Specific actions, not intentions)
2. What credibility did I damage yesterday? (Be brutally honest)
3. What authentication gap will I close today? (One concrete action)

Please write it down. Every day. This isn't journaling. This is system monitoring. You're checking the integrity of your most critical infrastructure: your own credibility. Remember, Chapter 2, authentication isn't about being liked. It's about being verified. This daily check ensures you're maintaining the three pillars: competence, consistency, and transparency.

When I was deployed, we ran system checks every morning without exception. Equipment failures in combat aren't inconvenient; they're fatal. The same applies to trust failures in organizations. They kill initiatives, destroy teams, and crater performance. Your morning authentication check is preventive maintenance on your most critical system.

The Vulnerability Acknowledgment (Real Time)

This one's harder because it requires you to override your instincts. Every time you feel defensive, every time you want to hide a mistake, every time you're tempted to spin a failure, stop. That's your moment.

Use the Vulnerability Map from Chapter 3. In real time, acknowledge what went wrong. Not in a self-flagellating way. Not in a performative way. In a systematic way:

- State the failure clearly
- Identify the impact
- Explain the correction
- Encrypt the lesson (protect what you learned so it compounds)

This should happen multiple times per week. If it's not, you're either perfect (you're not) or you're not being honest about your vulnerabilities. Remember: encryption isn't about hiding. It's about protecting what matters so it can grow stronger. Your vulnerabilities, properly encrypted and shared, become organizational antibodies.

I've watched leaders destroy their credibility by pretending to be invulnerable. I've watched others build legendary trust by systematically acknowledging failures and demonstrating learning. The difference isn't personality. It's protocol.

The Resilience Review (Weekly)

Every Friday, run your TIRS—Trust Incident Response Simulator. Not the full version you'd use in a crisis, but a quick diagnostic:

- What trust broke this week? (Even minor fractures)
- How did our systems respond?
- What would have happened without protocols in place?
- What needs hardening before next week?

This takes 15 minutes. Schedule it. Protect it. Make it as non-negotiable as your weekly security briefing. Because that's what it is, a security briefing for your organizational trust infrastructure.

Chapter 4 taught you that trust will break. The question isn't if, it's when and how prepared you are. This weekly review ensures you're not just reacting to trust failures, you're learning from them, hardening your systems, and building organizational resilience.

The Protocol Propagation (Daily)

Here's where most leaders fail: they build personal trust but don't systematize it. They become the bottleneck. Every decision flows through them. Every relationship depends on them. Every trust transaction requires their personal involvement.

That's not infrastructure. That's a single point of failure.

Daily, you must ask: What trust protocol did I propagate today? What system did I strengthen so it works without me? What process did I document so others can execute it? What cultural norm did I reinforce through my actions?

This is Chapter 6 in practice, trust as code. You're not just building trust. You're embedding it into systems that outlive your tenure, outscale your capacity, and operate independently of your personality.

In cybersecurity, we call this "defense in depth." Multiple layers of security so that if one fails, others hold. In trust infrastructure, it means building systems at every level: individual authentication, team encryption, organizational resilience, cultural firewalls, and automated protocols.

Every day, you should strengthen at least one layer.

The Human Firewall Reinforcement (Continuous)

Chapter 5 introduced the concept of culture as your human firewall, the collective immune system that detects and responds to threats to trust. But firewalls require constant updating. New threats emerge. New vulnerabilities appear. New attack vectors develop.

Your job is continuous reinforcement. This isn't a program you launch. It's a discipline you maintain.

When you see someone demonstrate trust-building behavior, name it specifically. When you see someone violate protocol, address it immediately. When you see a gap in your cultural defenses, close it systematically.

This is where most "trust initiatives" fail. They treat culture change as a campaign with a beginning and an end. But your human firewall isn't a campaign. It's your immune system. It requires daily nourishment, constant vigilance, and immediate response to threats.

Every interaction is an opportunity to strengthen or weaken your human firewall. Every meeting. Every email. Every decision. You're either reinforcing or undermining the protocols. There's no neutral.

Leading Through Protocol, Not Personality

Let's address the elephant in the room: this approach feels mechanical to some leaders. They worry it lacks warmth, humanity, and authenticity. They've been taught that leadership is about charisma, about inspiring through personality, about being the kind of person others want to follow.

That's not wrong. It's just insufficient.

And more importantly, it's not scalable.

I've seen charismatic leaders build incredible teams. I've also seen those teams collapse the moment that the leader left. I've seen inspiring personalities create devoted followers. I've also seen those organizations struggle to function without constant personal intervention from the top.

Personality-driven leadership has a fatal flaw: it doesn't transfer. It doesn't scale. It doesn't survive succession. It creates dependency, not capability.

Protocol-driven leadership does the opposite.

When you lead through protocol, you're not diminishing your humanity. You're multiplying your impact. You're building systems that work when you're not in the room. You're creating infrastructure that survives your departure. You're establishing standards that don't depend on your personal presence to maintain.

Think about the difference:

Personality-driven leadership says, "Trust me because of who I am."

Protocol-driven leadership says, "Trust this system because of how it works."

Personality-driven leadership asks: "How can I inspire people to trust?"

Protocol-driven leadership asks: "How can I build systems that generate trust?"

Personality-driven leadership measures: "Do people like me? Do they believe in me?"

Protocol-driven leadership measures: "Are the protocols working? Are the systems resilient? Is trust infrastructure operational?"

This isn't about being cold or mechanical. Some of the most effective protocol-driven leaders I've known were also deeply warm, genuinely caring people. But they understood something crucial: their warmth was a feature, not the foundation. The foundation was the system.

In Chapter 7, we explored how AI and automation are forcing this evolution. As organizations scale, as decisions accelerate, and as complexity increases, personality-driven leadership cannot keep pace. You cannot personally authenticate every relationship. You cannot personally encrypt every vulnerable moment. You cannot personally respond to every trust incident.

But your protocols can.

When you embed trust into systems, you create something remarkable: leadership that scales exponentially. Your authentication protocols work in every team, not just the ones you personally lead. Your vulnerability practices spread through culture, not just through your example. Your resilience systems activate automatically, not just when you're present to trigger them.

This is the competitive advantage that most organizations miss. While they're trying to hire more charismatic leaders, you're building a trust infrastructure that makes every leader more effective. While they're running trust workshops and motivation seminars, you're hardening systems that automatically generate trust.

Here's what this looks like in practice:

You walk into a meeting. Instead of relying on your personal credibility to drive decisions, you reference the authentication protocols everyone understands. Instead of using your charisma to smooth over conflicts, you activate the vulnerability practices embedded in your culture. Instead of personally mediating every trust issue, you point to the resilience systems that handle them systematically.

You're still present. You're still leading. But you're leading through infrastructure, not personality. And that infrastructure continues working long after you leave the room.

This Is What I Mean When I Say: You Are the Protocol

Not because you're mechanical or impersonal. But because you've so thoroughly embedded trust protocols into your leadership that they're inseparable from how you operate. You don't think about authentication; you authenticate naturally. You don't remember to be vulnerable; vulnerability is your default. You don't try to build resilience; resilient systems are how you work.

The protocol isn't something you do. It's something you are.

And here's the beautiful part: when you lead this way, you give everyone else permission to do the same. You're not creating a cult of personality around yourself. You're building a culture of protocol around trust. You're not making people dependent on your leadership. You're making them capable of leading themselves.

That's sustainable. That's scalable. That's the kind of leadership that actually transforms organizations.

The Real Legacy of a Leader

Let me tell you what legacy isn't.

It's not the speeches people remember. It's not the awards on your wall. It's not the revenue you generated or the market share you captured. It's not even the people you mentored or the careers you launched.

Those things matter. But they're not legacy.

Legacy is what works after you're gone.

Legacy is the systems that continue operating. The protocols are being executed. The infrastructure that remains standing. The trust that persists without your personal maintenance.

I learned this in the military, where legacy is measured by the lives saved by the systems you built, and where the protocols you established continue to protect people long after you've rotated out. Where the infrastructure you hardened keeps functioning through conditions you never anticipated.

The same principle applies to organizational leadership.

Your real legacy is the trust infrastructure you leave behind. Not the trust people had in you personally, but the trust systems that function independently of you. Not the relationships you built, but the relationship protocols you established. Not the crises you personally resolved, but the crisis response systems you created.

This reframes everything about how you lead.

Instead of asking "How can I be more trustworthy?" you ask "How can I build more trustworthy systems?"

Instead of focusing on "What do people think of me?" you focus on "What systems will outlive me?"

Instead of measuring "How much trust have I built?" you measure "How much trust infrastructure have I created?"

Let me make this concrete with the frameworks you've learned:

Your Authentication Legacy isn't that people trusted your competence; it's that they trusted your competence. It's that you established competence standards that persist. It's the verification protocols that continue authenticating credibility. It's the transparency systems that keep operating. When you leave, does authentication still happen? That's your legacy.

Your Encryption Legacy isn't about being vulnerable. It's that you normalized vulnerability as protocol. It's the psychological safety systems you embedded. It's the protection mechanisms you built around what matters most. When you leave, can people still be vulnerable safely? That's your legacy.

Your Resilience Legacy isn't that you handled crises well. It's that you built crisis response systems that work without you. It's the TIRS protocols that activate automatically. It's the organizational antibodies that respond to threats to trust. When you leave, does the organization recover from trust failures? That's your legacy.

Your Human Firewall Legacy isn't that you built a great culture. It's that you embedded cultural protocols that self-reinforce. It's the immune system that detects and responds to threats. It's the collective capability that doesn't depend on your presence. When you leave, does the culture maintain itself? That's your legacy.

Your Trust-as-Code Legacy isn't about making good decisions. It's that you systematized decision-making so others can make good decisions. It's the embedded protocols that guide behavior. It's the automated systems that scale trust. When you leave, do the systems keep working? That's your legacy.

This is hard for many leaders to accept because it requires ego death. It requires accepting that your personal indispensability is, in fact, organizational vulnerability. It requires building yourself out of the critical path. It requires creating systems that make you less necessary, not more.

But this is the only kind of leadership that actually matters.

I think about the leaders I served under in Afghanistan. The ones I remember most aren't the ones with the most prominent personalities or the most inspiring speeches. They're the ones who built systems that kept us alive. The ones who established protocols that worked when everything went wrong. The ones who created infrastructure that functioned under conditions they never anticipated.

Those leaders understood something profound: in high-stakes environments, personality is a luxury. Protocol is survival.

Your organization might not face life-or-death situations. But it faces trust-or-collapse situations constantly. And in those moments, your personality won't save you. Your protocols will.

So build them. Harden them. Test them. Refine them. Embed them so deeply into your organization that they become invisible, not because they're absent, but because they're so fundamental that everyone takes them for granted.

That's legacy.

That's what remains when you're gone.

That's what actually matters.

The Turn Ahead

We're back where we started: late at night, facing a turn that seems wrong.

But now you understand what I didn't understand then. The GPS didn't earn my trust through charisma. It earned my trust through protocol. Through consistent authentication. Through encrypted reliability. Through resilient performance across hundreds of previous turns.

When it told me to turn left, I didn't trust it unquestioningly. I was trusting systematically. I was trusting the infrastructure that had proven itself through rigorous testing and consistent performance.

That's what you're building in your organization.

Not blind trust. Not personality-dependent trust. Not hope-based trust.

Systematic trust. Infrastructure-based trust. Protocol-driven trust.

And here's what that means for you, right now, today:

You have a choice to make. You can close this book and go back to leading the way you've always led: through personality, through charisma, through personal intervention in every trust transaction. That works until it doesn't. It scales until it can't. It survives until you leave.

Or you can make a different choice.

You can start building trust infrastructure today. Not someday. Not when conditions are perfect. Today.

You can run your morning authentication check tomorrow. You can acknowledge your vulnerability in real time. You can schedule your weekly resilience review. You can propagate one protocol. You can reinforce your human firewall in your next interaction.

You can start leading through protocol, not personality.

You can start building a legacy that matters.

You can become the protocol.

Because here's the truth that every cybersecurity professional knows, that every military operator understands, that every systems thinker recognizes: the protocol doesn't care about your feelings. It doesn't care about your intentions. It doesn't care about your personality, charisma, or inspiring vision.

The protocol cares about one thing: does it work?

When trust breaks, and it will break, does your system respond? When crises hit, and they will, does your infrastructure hold? When you're not in the room, and you won't always be in the room, do your protocols keep executing?

That's the only question that matters.

And you already know the answer. You know whether your current approach is building infrastructure or just building dependency. You know whether you're creating systems or just creating the illusion of trust. You know whether you're hardening protocols or just hoping personality will be enough.

You know.

So now you have to decide: What are you going to do about it?

The frameworks are in your hands. The tools are at your disposal. The protocols are ready for implementation. The only variable left is you.

Will you be the leader who talks about trust? Or the leader who builds trust infrastructure?

Will you be the kind of person people remember? Or the protocol that keeps working?

Will you be the bottleneck? Or the architect of systems that scale beyond you?

The turn is ahead. It looks wrong. Your instincts are screaming. Everything in you wants to rely on what's comfortable, what's familiar, what's always worked before.

But the GPS says to turn left.

The protocol is telling you to build infrastructure.

The system is telling you that trust isn't a feeling, it's a framework.

And you are the protocol.

So turn left.

Build the systems.

Harden the infrastructure.

Embed the protocols.

Become the kind of leader whose legacy isn't measured in personal achievements but in organizational capability. Become the type of leader who doesn't just build trust but builds trust-building systems. The kind of leader who understands that the highest form of leadership isn't being indispensable, it's building infrastructure that makes you unnecessary.

That's the turn ahead.

That's your protocol.

That's your legacy.

Now execute.

List of Abbreviations

AI	artificial intelligence
CISO	chief information security officer
COO	chief operating officer
CTO	chief technology officer
DACI	driver, approver, contributors, informed
GPS	global positioning system
HR	human resources
IT	information technology
NASA	national aeronautics and space administration
NIST	national institute of standards and technology
QA	quality assurance
RAPID	recommend, agree, perform, input, decide
SaaS	software as a service
TIRS	trust incident response simulator
TMI	too much information
VP	vice president

Glossary

Accountability: clarity of ownership and responsibility
AI trust framework: checklist for evaluating trustworthiness of AI systems
Accessibility: ease of engaging with a system or process
Accept zone: low likelihood, low impact trust areas
Antifragility: becoming stronger through stress or adversity
Authentication: process of verifying identity and credibility
Automation complacency: over-reliance on automation causing human skill decay
Bias audit: review to identify fairness issues in data or models
Bias red team: group tasked with actively finding bias or system flaws
Bias risk: potential for inequitable outcomes in automated systems
Commander's intent: clarity of objective guiding decisions
Commitment audit: review of alignment between intentions, values, and actions
Consistency: reliability of outcomes given similar inputs
Critical zone: high likelihood and high impact trust vulnerabilities
Culture temperature: measurement of perceived safety, trust, and clarity
Empathy simulation: false display of emotional intelligence
Explainability: ability to articulate why a system made a decision
Future Risk Matrix: tool for assessing automated system risks

Human firewall: people acting as frontline trust defenders
Impact risk: degree to which decisions significantly affect people
Innovation impostor: innovation language masking risk-averse behavior
Learning (system): ability to capture and act on feedback
Monitor zone: high likelihood, low impact vulnerabilities
Multi-factor: security method using multiple verification elements
Prepare zone: low likelihood, high impact potential events
Privilege escalation: accessing authority beyond legitimate scope
Protocol propagation: embedding trust into systems daily
Protocol Scorecard: tool for evaluating trustworthiness of systems
Resilience grid: mapping of trust likelihood and impact
Resilience review: weekly evaluation of trust failures and strengths
Session hijacking: taking credit or access belonging to someone else
Servant leadership (false): service language masking self-interest
Transparency: clarity of rules and criteria
Transparency risk: inability to explain or audit system logic
Transparency theater: appearance of openness without true disclosure
Trust assets: systems that reliably build trust
Trust breach: breakdown in trust that causes harm
Trust gaps: areas where trust is undermined or inconsistent
Trust infrastructure map: visual showing trust strengths and weaknesses
Trust opportunities: small changes that increase trust quickly
Trust risks: vulnerabilities that could lead to trust failures
TIRS: Trust Incident Response Simulator
Values alignment: consistency between systems and stated values
Vulnerability map: tool for acknowledging and processing failures
Zero trust: model requiring continuous verification of every user and action

Index

A

B

C

D

E

For Product Safety Concerns and Information please contact our EU representative GPSR@taylorandfrancis.com
Taylor & Francis Verlag GmbH, Kaufingerstraße 24, 80331 München, Germany

www.ingramcontent.com/pod-product-compliance
Ingram Content Group UK Ltd.
Pitfield, Milton Keynes, MK11 3LW, UK
UKHW020206200926
475702UK00004B/632

* 9 7 8 1 0 4 1 1 7 2 6 6 6 *